BAKELESS SWEETS

PUDDING // PANNA COTTA //
FLUFF // ICEBOX CAKE //
AND MORE NO-BAKE DESSERTS

FAITH DURAND

PHOTOGRAPHS // STACY NEWGENT

BAKELESS SWEETS

PUDDING // PANNA COTTA //
FLUFF // ICEBOX CAKE //
AND MORE NO-BAKE DESSERTS

FAITH DURAND

STEWART, TABORI & CHANG
NEW YORK

Published in 2013 by Stewart, Tabori & Chang
An imprint of ABRAMS

Library of Congress Cataloging-in-Publication Data:

Durand, Faith.
 Bakeless sweets : pudding, panna cotta, fluff, icebox cake, and more no-bake desserts / By Faith Durand.
    pages cm
 Includes index.
 ISBN 978-1-61769-014-3
1. Desserts. 2. Quick and easy cooking. 3. Cookbooks. lcgft I. Title.
 TX773.D823 2013
 641.86—dc23
                     2012035639

Editor: Natalie Kaire
Designer: Amy Sly
Production Manager: Tina Cameron
Food Styling: Simon Andrews
Prop Styling: Deborah Williams

The text of this book was composed in Neutraface Text and Sentinel

Printed and bound in China

10 9 8 7 6 5 4 3 2 1

Stewart, Tabori & Chang books are available at special discounts when purchased in quantity for premiums and promotions as well as fundraising or educational use. Special editions can also be created to specification. For details, contact specialsales@abramsbooks.com or the address below.

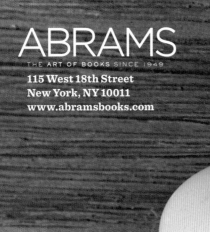

ABRAMS
THE ART OF BOOKS SINCE 1949

115 West 18th Street
New York, NY 10011
www.abramsbooks.com

introduction

I *love* pudding. Given an option, I'll always choose the creamy thing to be eaten off a spoon. My favorite desserts are all spoonful sweets—butterscotch pudding, silky chocolate mousse, tiramisu, and peach jelly made with real fruit.

It seems there is a cookbook for nearly everything these days, so imagine my surprise when I discovered that there was no one-stop shop for spoonful desserts, no single cookbook that gathered these sweets into one place. I could find no pudding cookbooks—and very few no-bake cookbooks—and certainly nothing that included everything from homey pudding to elegant panna cotta to crowd-pleasing icebox cake.

I wanted that book on my shelf, so I wrote it.

WHY NO-BAKE DESSERTS?

This book contains desserts that spend no time in the oven. Even the pie crusts in the icebox desserts chapter are no-bake. Why? Because it often seems like baked desserts get all the attention, and I wanted to throw this easy, pleasurable category of sweets its very own party. My favorite sort of dessert—pudding—is mostly a no-bake proposition. And although there are custards, rice puddings, and pots de crème that *are* baked, you won't find any of those in this book.

NO MORE PUDDING POWDERS OR JELL-O BOXES!

Puddings and fruit jellies are treats heavily associated with boxed mixes and preflavored powders. This is a bit silly, as people were making these homey sweets long before instant pudding in a box existed. I wanted to show how easy making pudding from scratch can be and inspire you to never buy another box of instant pudding.

The same for fruit gelatin: Why use Jell-O from a box when you could make it just as easily from natural fruit juice thickened with plain gelatin?

If you've ever eaten a chic dish of panna cotta at a restaurant you have probably sighed over its silky texture and wished you could make it at home. You can! Home cooks need to see how simple many restaurant-style desserts actually are, so I offer several varieties of panna cotta, mousse, and other so-called fancy desserts. The little secret of restaurant pastry kitchens is that these rich puddings are actually among the easiest, quickest desserts known to man or woman.

A DIVERSE WEALTH OF BAKELESS SWEETS

No-bake desserts showcase a wide variety of sweets from around the world, sweets that go beyond traditional Western cookies and cakes. They include candy, like marshmallows and brittle, and stovetop desserts from India, Thailand, China, and other cuisines, as most non-Western cultures don't traditionally use ovens. No-bake desserts could also include simple uncooked fruit platters, as well as desserts that may leave *your* oven cold but call for baked store-bought goods, like meringues or crackers.

The category of desserts that do not spend any time in the oven is so vast that there simply wasn't room to include them all! So my task here was to look for recipes *I* loved. This is a book for me, first of all. I have extensively tasted and love each and every recipe in this book. I also talked with some of my fellow home cooks and cookbook authors, asking them for memories and good tips, seeking out their favorite homey stovetop desserts.

DESSERTS TO CLOSE A MEAL

I also only chose recipes that really can stand on their own as desserts. Personally, I consider most candies and brittles to be snacks or treats to be eaten between meals or under the Christmas tree, not desserts to close a meal. So with one or two exceptions, you won't find candy or sugarcraft here. Icebox cakes enjoy huge popularity (I have observed this firsthand!), so you'll find some seriously crowd-pleasing pudding cakes. And I couldn't leave out other classic chilled desserts such as tiramisu, Eton Mess, and fruit trifle.

"PUDDING? I *LOVE* PUDDING!"

This seems to be the nearly unanimous response to any mention of the word *pudding*. People have nostalgic and happy memories of pudding, whether it came in a Snack Pack cup or out of their grandmother's copper saucepan.

PUDDING AND HEALTH

I realize we live in a health-conscious age, but this is not a "health" cookbook. You'll find plenty of heavy cream, whole milk, and sugar in these pages. I make no apologies for this; in fact, I insist on using full-fat dairy most of the time. Why? Because it tastes better and is more satisfying. Personally, I believe that it is healthier to eat a spoonful or two of something deeply satisfying than a whole bowl of an insipid low-fat creation. An indulgent pudding can be extremely pleasurable in small doses. In fact, many of these puddings should be served in tiny cups for savoring in small quantities.

But on the whole, this is a book for people who enjoy cream and sweet things, and who aren't averse to a spoonful of something truly, utterly *delicious* from time to time.

GLUTEN-FREE EATING

Most of the puddings and no-bake desserts in this book are naturally gluten-free, so if you eat gluten-free, I hope you see this as a delightful resource.

One caveat: If you eat gluten-free, you know that avoiding flour isn't your only task in the kitchen. Many otherwise gluten-free ingredients, from raisins to cornstarch to spices, are contaminated with gluten, which is inadvertently introduced during processing. So if you are avoiding gluten or cooking for someone who is, please always double-check your ingredients, and when in doubt, buy certified gluten-free products.

THE VEGAN DIET
Dairy

A pudding book isn't the best place for vegan dessert options, as nearly every recipe does contain dairy. I have, however, given some thought to making a few of these desserts friendly to vegans and to those who cannot eat dairy for health reasons. There are some recipes in this book that use almond milk or coconut milk. There is also a whole chapter of fruit jellies, most of which do not have any dairy. For a list of dairy-free (and vegan-friendly) desserts, see page 14.

Gelatin

All puddings are vegetarian, right? Well, not so fast! Vegans and many strict vegetarians avoid gelatin, which is an animal by-product. There is no perfect vegetarian substitute yet for gelatin, which is firm when cold and melts pleasantly in the mouth when warmed to body temperature. Vegetable and seaweed alternatives are usually chewier and occasionally trickier to work with. But again, I've given some attention to gelatin alternatives for vegetarians and for cooks who keep kosher. See the gelatin section, beginning on page 95, for more on gelatin and substitutes.

FIVE REASONS TO EAT MORE PUDDING AND NO-BAKE DESSERTS

Here are five reasons why I think pudding and no-bake desserts should get a lot more love.

1. **Speed:** Pudding is *quick*—quicker than most baked goods. You don't need to haul out a mixer and flour canisters. Many puddings can be made in fifteen minutes flat and, if you eat them warm, can be completely ready in a mere half hour.

2. **Convenience:** Have you ever noticed how nearly every nice restaurant has a panna cotta or mousse on its dessert menu? Pastry chefs understand that pudding desserts are *great* when made ahead. Unlike cake, which can be stale after a day, pudding or mousse holds very well in the fridge for several days. How convenient!

3. **Whole Grains:** Whole grains are having their day, with quinoa, millet, and other yummy—and, until recently, largely unknown—seeds and grains entering cooks' repertoires. If you're interested in these whole grains, then pudding is an easy way to enjoy them. Rather than try to adapt a baked good to whole-wheat flour or millet, make a pudding and get full-on taste (and fiber). It's also a great way to get your kids to eat more whole grains.

4. **Less Sugar:** In baking, sugar plays a complex role. It's there for sweetness, yes, but it also adds moistness and tenderness. Play with the sugar content in a cake at your own risk. Want to substitute a sugar-free sweetener or agave syrup? Not so fast—you may find yourself with a flop. But pudding is different. You can greatly reduce sugar or substitute sugar alternatives much more freely. In fact, some puddings and desserts in this book contain no refined sugar at all and depend only on honey or fruit juice for sweetness.

5. **Nostalgic Pleasure:** Puddings and no-bake desserts offer their own unique pleasure. Butterscotch pudding licked from a spoon or rice pudding eaten warm with cinnamon: Both evoke a nostalgic pleasure for childhood and old-fashioned desserts. Everyone loves pudding—why not make it more often?

PUDDINGS FOR EVERY OCCASION

Looking for something in particular? A recipe for a holiday or a dietary restriction? Here are ten lists to help guide you to a recipe that suits you! (And remember, nearly every recipe in this book is gluten-free, which is why I didn't include a separate list of gluten-free recipes.)

10 QUICKEST RECIPES

Don't have much time? The recipes in this list keep the hands-on time and chilling time to a minimum.

1 Rich Vanilla Pudding (page 32)
2 Simple Chocolate Pudding (page 34)
3 Stovetop Rice Pudding (with Uncooked Rice) (page 74)
4 Quicker Tapioca Pudding (page 88)
5 Vanilla Panna Cotta (page 104)
6 Deepest Chocolate Mousse (page 127)
7 Easy and Light Peach Blender Mousse (page 128)
8 Basic Fruit Jellies (page 139)
9 Strawberry-Rhubarb Fool (page 170)
10 Strawberry Eton Mess (page 198)

10 CHOCOLATE RECIPES

Craving chocolate? Start here.

1 Simple Chocolate Pudding (page 34)
2 Rich Chocolate Custard (page 36)
3 Malted Milk Pudding with Hot Fudge Sauce (page 44)
4 Chocolate-Butterscotch Budino (page 67)
5 Dark Chocolate and Rosewater Rice Pudding (page 79)
6 Milky Chocolate Panna Cotta (page 107)
7 Deepest Chocolate Mousse (page 127)
8 Nutella Fluff (page 175)
9 Triple Chocolate Cream Icebox Cake (page 184)
10 Oreo Icebox Pie (page 194)

10 PUDDINGS TO EAT WARM

Most puddings and desserts in this book are chilled and eaten cold from the fridge. Here are ten that are best eaten warm, shortly after cooking.

1 Maple-Bourbon Budino with Spiced Pecans (page 62)
2 Chocolate-Butterscotch Budino (page 67)
3 Stovetop Rice Pudding (with Uncooked Rice) (page 74)
4 Arroz con Tres Leches (page 77)
5 Salted Caramel Risotto (page 80)

6 Old-Fashioned Tapioca Pudding (page 86)

7 Thai Sticky Rice with Mango and Sesame Seeds (page 85)

8 Gingered Brown Rice Pudding with Plum Conserve (page 82)

9 Coffee, Almond, and Date Millet Pudding (page 92)

10 Spicy Peanut and Toasted Coconut Cookies (page 203)

10 EGG-FREE RECIPES

There are plenty of puddings that don't include eggs (see the entire panna cotta chapter, starting on page 94). Here are ten egg-free recipes from other sections of the book.

1 Simple Vanilla Pudding (page 28)

2 Simple Chocolate Pudding (page 34)

3 Stovetop Rice Pudding (with Uncooked Rice) (page 74)

4 Salted Caramel Risotto (page 80)

5 Coconut-Ricotta Mousse with Pistachio and Pomegranate (page 134)

6 Papaya Filled with Coconut Cream and Mango (page 152)

7 Strawberry-Rhubarb Fool (page 170)

8 Blood Orange Fluff with Chocolate Shavings (page 176)

9 No-Bake Lemon Cheesecake with Blueberry Sauce (page 195)

10 Lemon Cream Icebox Cake (page 183)

10 RECIPES FOR A BIG CROWD

The recipes in this book are mostly sized in modest quantities of four to eight servings, but some of the icebox desserts are best made for a crowd. Here are ten recipes to consider when you need a dessert for a bigger group.

1 Cara Cara Orange Mousse (page 132)

2 Holiday Cranberry Gelatin Mold (page 147)

3 The Ultimate Banana Pudding Parfait (page 197)

4 Chocolate and Vanilla Trifle with Caramel Sauce (page 199)

5 Blueberry Angel Food Trifle (page 200)

6 Spiced Rum and Pumpkin Trifle (page 199)

7 Lemon Cream Icebox Cake (page 183)

8 Triple Chocolate Cream Icebox Cake (page 184)

9 S'mores Pudding Cake (page 189)

10 Gingersnap and Cinnamon Icebox Cupcakes (page 186)

10 RECIPES FOR SPRING

These are recipes for spring—redolent of lemon, lavender, early berries, and mint.

1 Garden Mint and Cocoa Pudding (page 35)

2 Lemon and Sour Cream Custard (page 52)

3 Creamy Lemon-Coconut Quinoa Pudding (page 90)

4 Honey-Lavender Panna Cotta (page 105)

5 Strawberry-Yogurt Panna Cotta (page 113)

10 RECIPES FOR SUMMER

Puddings for summer—cold jellies and the flavors of peaches, lemonade, and basil.

10 RECIPES FOR FALL

Sweeter, richer recipes with warm spices and chocolate are just right for fall.

10 RECIPES FOR WINTER

Winter means colder days and longer nights, and so warm, indulgent puddings are called for. This is the time to break out the classics and to impress your date on Valentine's Day.

10 DAIRY-FREE RECIPES

A pudding book isn't the logical place to look for dairy-free recipes (hello, cream!), and I'll be the first to admit that dairy substitutes are not my primary area of expertise. But there are quite a few dairy-free recipes in this book, mostly in the form of fruit jellies (see page 137). There are others as well that are either dairy-free or offer a dairy-free option—here's a sampling.

KITCHEN EQUIPMENT

One of the pleasures of pudding and no-bake desserts is that they can be made with very little special equipment. You'll want a **heavy saucepan**, with a thick bottom to help keep milk from scorching. It's nice if you have a 3-quart (2.8-L) saucepan, as it gives you a little more room to work with, but a 2-quart (2-L) will do for most of the recipes here. You can always use a bigger pot in a pinch.

Make sure you have a **whisk**; a big balloon-style whisk is indispensable when making pudding and fruit jellies. I also like to have a smaller whisk on hand for making slurries, as well as a flat-bottomed whisk for getting the last lumps out.

All right—my husband is giving me an admonishing look—who am I kidding? I'm addicted to whisks. I think I have at least nine different sorts squirreled away. But these aren't essential. My point is, just make sure you have some sort of whisk. I can tell you, from regretful personal experience, that when it comes to pudding, a fork is *not* a substitute for a good whisk.

I do call for two things that you may not have. **A stand mixer** or **electric hand mixer** is useful for whipping cream for icebox cakes and pies and for topping puddings, although you can beat cream by hand, too. (It's a great workout and doesn't take as long as you might think.) A large—6 inches (15 cm) or more across—**fine-mesh sieve** is also called for in a few recipes for straining pudding or gelatin mixtures.

You probably already have a 9-by-13-inch (23-by-33-cm) baking pan, wooden or plastic spoons for stirring, and a big mixing bowl or two. They are all essential.

(If you want a little more help or direction on tools, refer to the last section of this book. There you'll find more detail and sources for ingredients and equipment, as well as a list of books I referenced while writing this one.)

GOOD THINGS FOR SERVING

Here are a few of the serving dishes you might want to have on hand: shallow glass or plastic **2-quart (2-L) containers** for storing puddings and jellies and helping them cool quickly, a **9-inch (23-cm) pie pan** for making icebox pies, and a deep glass bowl or **trifle dish** for trifles and Eton Mess.

Many pudding and panna cotta desserts are best when chilled and served in individual portions, so if you have six to eight **4- or 6-ounce (120- or 180-ml) ramekins** or small bowls around, then you'll put them to good use. And since everything is cuter when served in a jar, don't forget about **wide-mouth 1/2-pint or 250-ml canning jars**.

Of course, if you're really into pudding, you'll soon be casting an acquisitive gaze toward glass cups and dessert dishes of all sorts. Watch out—puddingware can be addictive! And let's not even begin talking about spoons. Look in the Sources section (page 213) for ideas for pretty spoons for eating and serving.

INGREDIENTS

I'll speak more extensively on ingredients in each chapter, depending on the type of pudding we're working with. But let me sum up a few important points here:

Milk These recipes were tested with homogenized, ultra-pasteurized, whole milk (3.25 percent or greater fat content). The milk is the dominant ingredient in many of these puddings, so use the best you can. I usually opt for organic.

Cream I used homogenized, ultra-pasteurized, heavy cream (36 percent or greater butterfat) in the pudding and panna cotta recipes. I tend to avoid cream marked specifically as "whipping" cream, since this often has more stabilizers and gums added.

Light Cream The recipes are formulated for heavy cream, but light cream (30 to 35 percent butterfat) *can* be substituted. It may take a little longer to whip, and it will stay softer when used for whipped cream and icebox cakes.

Shelf-Stable Milk You can use shelf-stable (aseptic) milk (such as Parmalat or Organic Valley) as long as it is still whole milk. The taste of shelf-stable milk can be slightly different than refrigerated milk, however, and not everyone prefers it.

Sweetened Condensed Milk Milk cooked down with sugar. It's thick and syrupy and should not be confused with evaporated milk, which is not sweetened at all.

Eggs I use large eggs in these recipes.

Sugar Fine white granulated sugar. Beet and cane sugar are both equally good choices.

Salt These recipes call for two different kinds of salt: table salt and kosher salt. Fine table salt is used most frequently; this is the common table salt (referred to simply here as "salt") that we stir into puddings and cookies to flavor the whole batch. Kosher salt is chunkier and rougher and is used to season some of the toppings and brittles where I want a pop of salt that crunches.

Vanilla Vanilla extract is an important ingredient and I recommend pure vanilla extract. My personal favorite is Nielsen-Massey's Mexican vanilla extract; it has a deep, spicy flavor. For economy, I buy it in large bottles and funnel it into a smaller bottle.

Vanilla Beans Some recipes call for whole vanilla beans. These are quite expensive, and it takes a little extra work to incorporate them into a pudding. So I call for them only in puddings where the full-bodied richness of real vanilla bean will make a crucial difference to the recipe. In desserts where vanilla plays more of a supporting role, extract is just fine.

HOMOGENIZED, ULTRA-PASTEURIZED DAIRY

These recipes are formulated for homogenized, ultra-pasteurized milk and cream. This may seem obvious, but I emphasize it because more and more cooks have access now to nonhomogenized milks, sometimes pasteurized at lower temperatures. Personally, I like to buy milk and cream from a local dairy that does not homogenize it and pasteurizes it at the minimum mandated temperature. This means that the milk doesn't last as long in the fridge, but it tastes so much better. I did not, however, use this lovely stuff in testing the recipes for the book. I found that nonhomogenized milk tends to separate in cooked puddings, making them grainy and thinner than expected.

I also found that the cream from this dairy was much richer in fat than standard heavy whipping cream (which ranges from 36 to 40 percent butterfat). So my results would not have been consistent with those using standard store-bought ultra-pasteurized cream.

» The takeaway: These recipes are all formulated for homogenized, ultra-pasteurized milk and cream, and your results will be best when you stick to the recommended fat content.

STIRRED PUDDINGS & CUSTARDS

Plain vanilla pudding is the first sort of dessert many of us encounter as children. I have a hunch, though, that most kids think pudding like this comes out of a plastic cup or from a box of magic powder whisked into milk. But given how easy vanilla pudding is to make from scratch, there is room here for surprise and delight—you can make this stuff at home with no little box to help you, and it tastes *so* much better.

This chapter contains creamy old-fashioned puddings, thickened with cornstarch and eggs and made on top of the stove. Most of the classic puddings here can be made in just fifteen minutes, plus chilling time (if you like to eat your pudding firm and cold from the fridge).

We start with basic vanilla pudding, and build on that with more complex flavors: pumpkin spice with honey caramel, Nutella with hazelnut brittle, roasted pistachio, toasted coconut.

The flavors that work best in these cooked puddings are ones that stand up to longer cooking: darker, richer flavors like chocolate, butterscotch, caramel, vanilla, pistachio, pumpkin, spices. If you are looking for a creamy pudding with a brighter flavor like strawberry, mango, or another fruit, try a mousse or panna cotta instead; those methods are better for fresh fruit.

These puddings are not complicated. Let me tell you right here what you need in your fridge and pantry for homemade vanilla pudding: milk, cream, cornstarch, vanilla, and a bit of sugar. That's it. So put away that box and pick up a whisk!

BUDINO, CUSTARD, PASTRY CREAM: WHAT'S IN A NAME?

Puddings go by many names, and these can be interchangeable and confusing. Take *custard*. Some cooks consider *custard* a pudding with eggs that also happens to be baked. But in England *custard* is specifically a thin sauce of cream and eggs that is cooked on the stovetop and meant to be ladled over fruit or cake. And while we're in England, let's not forget that there the word *pudding* itself just means dessert! (Which leads to some confusion with my English friends when I say I am writing a book about pudding; I have to quickly explain that it's in the American sense, not in the more all-encompassing British meaning.)

Or take *budino*, which means "pudding" in Italian, but is sometimes taken to mean a baked pudding cake, and at other times an extra-rich pudding. I love the playful sound of the word, bouncing yet thick like a clotted pudding, so I have adopted it here to designate a collection of extra-rich puddings meant to be savored in very small quantities. I use a shot glass or a small ramekin to serve them. I like serving pudding in these tiny quantities at parties and after a luxurious dinner; they offer just a taste of something sweet, without overwhelming.

MILK, CREAM, AND FAT IN STOVETOP PUDDING

Dairy's role in thick and creamy puddings is very simple: Fat equals thickness. The fattier your dairy, the thicker and more luxurious your pudding will be. This is why I formulated these recipes for whole milk and why I do not recommend substituting skim or low-fat milk. Whole milk gives just the right amount of richness to these puddings.

Too much fat, however, can be as bad as too little. Puddings made with too much cream can be unpleasantly grainy, as the fat beads up and coats your tongue. So I try in each recipe to give the right balance of milk to cream for optimal eating pleasure.

>> **The takeaway:** Just trust me! Use whole milk and cream in these recipes—it's worth it.

ALTERNATIVE DAIRIES IN STOVETOP PUDDINGS

I found that the lower fat of soy, rice, and almond milk—not to mention their various reactions to heat—meant that alternative milks did not do well in the types of puddings in this chapter. Of course, you are free to experiment with alternative milks—but given that most of these recipes also depend on cream, I would again recommend that dairy-free cooks look to the grain pudding and panna cotta chapters, which contain a few dairy-free recipes and variations.

>> **The takeaway:** Dairy-free folks, don't despair! There are plenty of dairy-free recipes in later chapters! Grain pudding, panna cotta, and mousse are categories much better suited to dairy substitutes.

MAKING THICK AND CREAMY STOVETOP PUDDING

CORNSTARCH AND PUDDING

Cornstarch is a fine powdered starch made from corn that is used to thicken sauces and, in this case, puddings. It is tasteless, inexpensive, and easy to work with. It is not as powerful a thickener as arrowroot, but it is better for thickening dairy.

When working with cornstarch in puddings, there are two chief concerns: how to keep the mixture lump-free, since cornstarch likes to lump up when combined with liquid, and how long to boil the mixture, since cornstarch needs to be boiled in order to thicken. If you do not boil cornstarch long enough, it will not thicken at all or it will thicken then quickly separate after refrigeration.

>> To keep the pudding lump-free, whisk the cornstarch smooth in a small amount of liquid before adding it to the pudding. This is called **making a slurry**.

>> To thicken the cornstarch, I call for **two solid minutes** of boiling in most of the puddings. This should be timed from the moment the pudding comes to a full rolling boil, with numerous bubbles popping up to the surface. By this point, the pudding will have already begun to thicken. Allowing for two minutes of full rolling boil from this point on is enough to fully cook the cornstarch but not overcook it, which is also a danger if the pudding boils much too long (think five minutes, not two).

>> If you do get a lump or two of cornstarch in your finished pudding, you can **fix it** by straining the pudding through a fine-mesh sieve while it is still hot.

BASIC METHOD FOR CORNSTARCH PUDDING

Here's how to make a basic cornstarch pudding. Depending on the flavor and other elements, each pudding recipe may contain minor variations on this process, but this is the basic method.

1 **Make a cornstarch slurry:** Whisk together a little dairy and the cornstarch. The key to a silky pudding is to make this as smooth as possible—no lumps! Reach into the mixture with your fingertips and rub out lumps if you want to make sure it's really smooth. (If the pudding also calls for eggs or egg yolks, you will whisk them into this cornstarch slurry now.)

2 **Heat the dairy and sugar:** In a saucepan big enough to hold all the finished pudding (at least 2 quarts / 2 L), warm the rest of the dairy and the sugar over medium heat. Stir frequently to make sure the milk doesn't scorch.

3 **Temper the slurry:** When the sugar is dissolved and the dairy is hot (you should see the surface of the milk begin to vibrate—don't let it boil or you'll have a mess), pour a little bit of this hot milk into the slurry and whisk to combine really well.

4 **Thicken the pudding:** Pour this tempered mixture back into the pot slowly (count to ten as you pour) and whisk constantly. Now is when you get your arm workout for the day! Turn the heat up to medium-high and whisk, whisk, whisk. In one to five minutes, the pudding will begin to boil, with big, rolling *plops*, like little volcanoes exploding up to the surface. It will be getting thick by now. Keep whisking, and boil for a full two minutes from this point, turning down the heat a little if you are getting splattered with pudding. Don't go too far beyond the two-minute mark, however, as boiling the cornstarch too long can overcook it and make it get watery later.

5 **Flavor the pudding:** Now that the pudding is thick, turn off the heat and stir in vanilla, salt, or any other flavorings called for in the recipe.

6 **Chill the pudding:** Pour the pudding into a container and cover the surface completely with plastic wrap or buttered wax paper to keep it from drying out and forming a skin. Chill until the pudding is set and thick enough to eat. You can eat some puddings hot; others you'll want to let chill for a few hours.

EGGS IN PUDDING

Like cornstarch, eggs and egg yolks act as thickeners in a pudding. But while cornstarch simply thickens liquid and can have a grainy mouthfeel if too much is used, eggs add richness. Egg yolks make a pudding feel and taste more luxurious. The proteins in whole eggs also stabilize a pudding, helping it to maintain that thickness.

There are two problems in using eggs in puddings, however: curdling and an undesirably eggy taste.

» Curdling happens when eggs are heated too fast or overcooked. The protein in the egg separates out and forms unpleasantly firm strings and nubs of egg. To avoid this, it is best to **temper the eggs** before adding them to a pan of hot milk. To do this, stir a cupful of hot milk into the bowl of whipped eggs and cold cream. The hot liquid warms the eggs, but doesn't shock them.

» To avoid the eggy taste, I prefer to use more **egg yolks** than egg whites in puddings. While both parts of the egg have thickening power, the proteins in egg whites give off more eggy taste, and it is also easier for these to curdle, since they cook at a lower temperature.

» If the eggs in your pudding *do* curdle, no worries! You can **fix it**—just strain the pudding through a fine-mesh sieve while it's hot. If the pudding has already chilled, you can run an immersion blender through it quickly to help the eggs re-emulsify.

CHILLING PUDDING AND MAKING IT CREAMY AGAIN
HOW LONG TO CHILL PUDDING

I know, I know—it's hard to be patient after you've cooked up a delicious pudding, but most of them need to be chilled for at least a short amount of time so they are cool enough to eat, and some puddings won't be very thick at all until they have spent some time in the refrigerator.

I have tried to find the right texture, whether a pudding is eaten warm or cold. If you use a lot of fat, the pudding may be thick enough to eat almost immediately or after just a half hour in the refrigerator. But then it may turn out to be unpleasantly thick after it chills overnight.

Having said that, some puddings are best really cold (the Lemon and Sour Cream Custard on page 52, for instance), and others can be eaten warm (the Maple-Bourbon Budino on page 62 is best warm, even hot). Where applicable, I have noted the optimal serving temperature in the recipe.

Fortunately, when it comes to cooling, you do have some control over how long it will take. If you pour the pudding into a **wide and shallow dish**, it will cool much faster. In fact, when I'm really in a hurry, I spread a batch of pudding onto a jelly-roll pan so most of the pudding is exposed surface. There's just one thing to consider . . .

PUDDING SKIN!

How do you feel about pudding skin? It's that tender rubbery layer that materializes on top of a pudding in the refrigerator. This "skin" forms as the pudding dries out on top while it cools.

Some people detest it; others love it. Personally, I feel it's best to avoid it as your pudding chills for the first time, especially if you've spread it in a very wide and shallow dish. If you're not careful, half your pudding could be skin! (Of course, if this is your thing, go for it.)

To prevent a skin from forming, cover the surface of the warm pudding completely by placing plastic wrap or buttered wax paper directly on the surface.

ON EATING PUDDING AFTER REFRIGERATION

Once a pudding has set up in the fridge for a few hours, it will be thick and gelled. If you spoon it out of the container, it won't have that beautiful creaminess it did right out of the pot.

To make the pudding soft and creamy again, spoon it into a bowl and beat, either in a stand mixer fitted with the whisk attachment or with an electric hand mixer, just until the pudding is light and creamy. (Don't beat for more than a minute or so; it can cause the cornstarch's thickening power to break down.) You can also use a big balloon whisk. (I don't recommend using an immersion blender or regular blender, although a food processor could do in a pinch.)

HOW LONG DOES PUDDING LAST?

Personally, I feel that the puddings in this chapter are best eaten within three days. (If you can make them last that long!)

PUDDING TROUBLESHOOTING

Help! Something went wrong! Get your answers here.

» **My pudding is too thin!** Is it still warm? Most puddings need some time in the fridge to get really thick and creamy. Also, you may not have cooked the cornstarch long enough—it needs a full two minutes of boiling. On the other hand, if you lost track of time and wandered away, letting your pudding boil merrily for five or ten minutes, you may have *overcooked* the cornstarch, which has the same effect as undercooking. Also, I have calibrated most of these recipes to be best after some time in the fridge. If you like to eat your pudding warm, add one extra tablespoon of cornstarch to the recommended amount. This may add a touch more graininess, but it will help the pudding firm up faster.

» **My pudding thickened, but then got watery and separated in the fridge.** It's normal for cornstarch to leak a tiny bit of water, especially after several days of refrigeration. But if your pudding breaks down right away, that means you didn't cook the cornstarch long enough. Make sure you boil for a full two minutes.

» **Darn it! There are lumps in my pudding.** You need a better slurry. Make sure it's completely smooth and that you whisk vigorously when adding it to the warm dairy. If you notice lumps while the pudding is still hot, you can strain it through a fine-mesh sieve.

» **My pudding is too thick!** Did you use the recommended dairy? If you substituted cream for the milk or used a higher-fat cream, you may get an unpleasantly thick pudding. See the section about whipping cold pudding—you can make it silky and creamy again by whipping lightly with a mixer.

PUDDING IT ALL TOGETHER: SERVING TIPS AND IDEAS

» When you bring homemade pudding to the table, expect people to squeal. Homemade pudding is so pleasurable and unexpected, so comforting and delicious. A bowl of unadorned real vanilla pudding is always a treat, but there are ways to make pudding even more spectacular, especially for a special occasion.

SWEET SAUCES AND CRUNCHY TOPPINGS

Many of the recipes in this chapter and throughout the book have accompanying recipes for sauces and toppings, like brandied cherries, hazelnut brittle, and toasted coconut (you can see a full index of all the sauces and toppings in the book on page 218). Mix these up between flavors of pudding, or experiment with other toppings. I especially like crunchy, crumbly crust toppings on my pudding (the no-bake crusts used in the icebox pie recipes are great crumbled up as pudding toppings!). Here are a few favorite crunchy toppings:

» Crushed Oreos or Chocolate Sandwich Cookies

» Crushed Vanilla Wafers or Graham Crackers

» Toasted Coconut or Hazelnut Brittle (page 41 or 61)

» Toasted Nuts

» Baked Pie Dough or Puff Pastry Scraps Tossed with Cinnamon Sugar

» Toasted Bread Crumbs Tossed in Butter and Sugar

» Toasted Coconut (page 50)

» Toasted Rolled Oats

» Chocolate, Butterscotch, White Chocolate, Peanut Butter, or Cinnamon Chips

» Crushed Cornflakes or Other Cereal

» Crushed Meringues

» Chopped Pretzel Sticks

PUDDING JARS, VERRINES, AND PARFAIT FLAVOR COMBINATIONS

Plain pudding is well and good, especially when dressed up with the sauces and toppings in this chapter. But what if you want to really go all out and create a special treat?

If you visit a patisserie or sweets shop in France, you will find *verrines*, a fancy name for pudding cups, or what we might call parfaits. These are very popular and can be elaborately layered with cake cubes, fresh fruit, nuts, meringue, or many different flavors of pudding or custard. They are served in little glasses, a perfect small bite of sweet after a meal. Here are some ideas for making your very own chic verrines and pudding parfaits using various components from this book or from the grocery store (these are just a few ideas—I'm sure you can come up with plenty more!). Any would be adorable in a small Mason jar or pint glass, and some would be quite elegant in a tall Champagne flute.

To assemble the verrine, it's best to have your pudding mostly chilled. Then layer it in a cup or jar, smoothing as you go (or messy looks good too!) and adding mix-ins and sauces.

- » **Chai Latte Break** = Chai–White Chocolate Budino + Simple Vanilla Pudding + Whipped Cream + Sprinkle of Cardamom

- » **Salted Peppermint Patty** = Peppermint-Cocoa Pudding + Rich Vanilla Pudding + Crushed Pretzels + Crushed Peppermint Candy Bits

- » **Chocolate Lemon Bar** = Lemon and Sour Cream Custard + Rich Chocolate Custard + Graham Cracker Crumbs

- » **Mocha with a Kick** = Rich Mocha Pudding + Rich Vanilla Pudding + Splash of Bourbon + Whipped Cream

- » **Kid at Heart** = Rich Vanilla Pudding + Rich Chocolate Custard + Chocolate Cookie Crumbs + Hot Fudge Sauce + Gummy Worms

- » **Caramel Apple** = Butterscotch Pudding + Rich Vanilla Pudding + Buttered Apples + Caramel Sauce

- » **Twisted Black Forest** = No-Bake Crème Brûlée + Rich Chocolate Pudding + Brandied Cherry Sauce + Hot Fudge Sauce + Chopped Toasted Almonds

- » **Elvis Lives** = Banana Cream Pudding + Peanut Butter and Honey Pudding + Cooked Bacon Bits + Graham Cracker Crumbs

- » **Upside-Down Cake** = Pineapple Pudding + Caramel Pudding + Caramel Sauce + Coconut Brittle

- » **Nut-Lover's Delight** = Nutella Pudding + Roasted Pistachio Pudding + Whipped Cream + Spiced Pecans

- » **Classic American** = Cheesecake Budino + Rich Chocolate Custard + Hot Fudge Sauce + Whipped Cream + Fresh Strawberries

- » **PB&J** = Peanut Butter and Honey Pudding + Dollop of Jam + Crushed Pretzels

- » **Black Bottom Cake** = Cheesecake Budino + Rich Chocolate Custard + Whipped Mascarpone + Chocolate Chips

- » **Breakfast for Dessert** = Rich Vanilla Pudding + Simple Maple Pudding + Waffle Chunks (make a few extra and freeze, or buy your favorite frozen variety) + Maple Syrup Drizzle + Toasted Oats + Sprinkle of Cinnamon

MORE SWEET IDEAS FOR SERVING PUDDING

Sprinkled Pudding Spoons You can dispense with a cup or bowl entirely, and serve pudding spoons at a party. I like the soup spoons you can find at Asian groceries for this, since they hold more and can stand up on a plate. Fill each spoon with a bite of chilled, whipped pudding and shake sprinkles or drizzle sauce over them.

Chocolate Cup Pudding Shooters You can buy little cups made of chocolate or white chocolate at specialty cooking stores or online. Fill these with chilled, whipped pudding and let your guests eat the whole thing—cup and all!

Pudding Sundae Bar Make a big pot of vanilla or chocolate pudding, and set it out with bowls of sprinkles, chocolate shavings, crumbled crackers, fresh fruit, and other goodies and invite your guests to build their own pudding sundaes.

SIMPLE VANILLA PUDDING

Let's start at the very beginning: vanilla pudding. I call this simple vanilla pudding, but a better word would be elemental. It has only the most basic elements of pudding—milk, cornstarch, and sugar, flavored with salt and a dash of vanilla. This pudding is old-fashioned and gentle in its milky simplicity.

Ironically, it is tricky to make such a plain pudding; it is easier to make a richer one tarted up with eggs and cream. But I wanted to begin these recipes with the simplest pudding I know, a pudding good for young children and weeknight suppers. Use whole milk (this pudding won't be nearly as good made with lower-fat milk), and enjoy it as a delicious compromise between simplicity and flavor, the perfect weeknight treat.

MAKES 4 CUPS (960 ML)
OR EIGHT SERVINGS.
GLUTEN-FREE.

- 5 **tablespoons (40 g) cornstarch**
- ½ **teaspoon salt**
- 4 **cups (960 ml) whole milk, divided**
- 6 **tablespoons (75 g) sugar**
- 2 **teaspoons pure vanilla extract**
- 1 **tablespoon (14 g) unsalted butter, cut into several small chunks (optional)**

Make a cornstarch slurry: Put the cornstarch and salt in a medium bowl and whisk out any lumps. Slowly pour in 1 cup (240 ml) of the milk, whisking constantly. Whisk until there are no lumps in the mixture. (To be really sure, reach into the bowl and gently rub out any lumps between your fingers.)

Warm the milk over medium heat in a 2-quart (2-L) or larger saucepan. Whisk the sugar and remaining 3 cups (720 ml) milk together. (Resist the urge to turn the heat to high, as this puts you at a greater risk of scorching the milk. The higher the heat, the more attentive you should be.)

As the milk comes to a simmer, stir constantly but slowly with a wooden spoon, scraping the bottom of the pan evenly so that the milk doesn't scorch or form a thick skin on the bottom of the pan.

When the surface of the milk begins to quiver and vibrate, turn off the heat.

Temper the slurry: Pour 1 cup (240 ml) of the hot milk into the bowl with the slurry. Whisk them together, then pour the cornstarch mixture slowly back into the pan, counting to 10 as you do. Whisk vigorously to combine.

Thicken the pudding: Turn the heat back on to medium and bring the pudding to a boil, whisking frequently. When the milk begins to boil, you may not notice it at first, since large bubbles will rise very slowly, making a noise like *gloop* or *plop*. As this happens, the milk will thicken and become shiny and viscous. Let the pudding come to a rolling boil, which will take 2 to 5 minutes, with large bubbles popping up to the surface.

After the pudding comes to a rolling boil, reduce the heat to low and let the pudding simmer for 2 full minutes. Continue to stir or whisk gently but firmly.

Flavor the pudding: Turn off the heat and gently whisk in the vanilla. If you would like to add just a touch more richness, stir in the butter.

Chill the pudding: Immediately pour the hot pudding into a shallow container. (If you notice lumps in the pudding, you can pour it through a fine-mesh sieve to make it smoother.) Place plastic wrap or buttered wax paper directly on the surface of the pudding (if you don't like pudding skin). Put a lid on the dish and refrigerate it for 1 hour or until the pudding is completely cold before eating. Best eaten within 3 days.

EASY FLAVOR VARIATIONS
richer (yet still eggless) vanilla pudding

For a slightly richer pudding that still has no eggs, replace 1 cup (240 ml) of the whole milk with cream.

simple citrus pudding

Stir in 1 teaspoon lemon or orange zest instead of the vanilla extract. (For a zestier, tangier lemon pudding, try Lemon and Sour Cream Custard, page 52.)

simple cinnamon pudding

Stir in ½ teaspoon cinnamon, in addition to the vanilla extract.

simple maple pudding

Eliminate the sugar and stir in ¼ cup (60 ml) Grade B maple syrup (see Note, page 62) with the vanilla extract after the pudding has thickened.

TEMPERING A SLURRY

Why do we "temper" a slurry of cornstarch and egg yolks? This process helps to gradually warm up the eggs, preparing them to cook evenly and smoothly. It's like getting into a hot bath—it's more comfortable to add a little bit of hot water at a time rather than plunging immediately into very hot water. If you dropped beaten egg yolks straight into a hot pudding, they would curdle and form unpleasantly eggy lumps. Warming them, then gradually adding this prewarmed mixture to the hot pudding, helps the eggs incorporate smoothly into the pudding.

HOMEMADE INSTANT PUDDING MIX

Now that we've thoroughly dispelled the notion that you need a box of processed powder to make pudding at home, let's revisit the idea of a pudding mix. Did you know that you can make pudding mix from scratch, all by yourself? This pudding mix makes a fantastic holiday gift, packaged in a pretty jar and accompanied, perhaps, by a jar of Old-Fashioned Hot Fudge Sauce (page 45) or Honey Caramel Sauce (page 43).

This recipe depends on one specialty ingredient: ClearJel, a natural starch that has been modified to thicken instantly on contact with liquid, just like the puddings in the boxes. It is available two ways: instant and regular. Be sure to use the instant variety here. You can find ClearJel online or in baking specialty shops. You can also find it easily at any store catering to or run by Amish cooks; they use it extensively in baking pies.

What does homemade instant pudding taste like? It's sweet and milky, although definitely not as luxurious as a proper stovetop pudding. But it's pudding, and so quick and convenient—especially for making a pie or an icebox cake.

Make sure to use instant milk powder; non-instant will give this a gritty mouthfeel.

MAKES 2½ CUPS (600 ML) OR FIVE ½-CUP SERVINGS FINISHED PUDDING.

to prepare the mix

- ¼ cup (17 g) instant dry milk or instant malted milk powder
- ⅓ cup (53 g) Instant ClearJel
- 6 tablespoons (38 g) powdered sugar
- ½ teaspoon salt

to prepare pudding

- 2 cups (480 ml) cold whole milk

Whisk together the dry milk, ClearJel, sugar, and salt in a large bowl. Funnel into a clean, dry jar or airtight container for storage. This will keep for up to a year if stored in a cool place.

To prepare the pudding, dump the dry mix into a large bowl and slowly pour in the milk, beating with an electric hand mixer or immersion blender. The pudding will begin to thicken immediately, but will be thickest after it has been refrigerated for at least 10 minutes.

flavoring instant pudding mix

Here are a few ideas for flavoring your instant pudding mix.

» **Vanilla:** You can add vanilla when making the pudding, but you can also split open a vanilla bean and leave it in the pudding mix jar. This will flavor the whole batch. Another option is to use vanilla sugar, which is sugar flavored with vanilla beans or sugar that has been stored with a vanilla bean in the jar.

» **Cocoa:** For a cocoa pudding mix, add ¼ cup cocoa to the dry ingredients.

» **Spice:** Add ¼ teaspoon ground ginger and ¼ teaspoon cinnamon to the dry mix.

» **Freeze-dried fruit, ground to powder:** This is a fun way to flavor puddings. Take freeze-dried bananas or raspberries and grind them to a fine powder in the food processor. Add about ½ cup powder to a batch of pudding mix for color and flavor.

» **Other flavorings and colors:** Anything very dry and powdered can be added to this pudding mix to flavor or color it. Try adding powdered citrus, other spices, and natural coloring agents like beet powder.

// SIMPLE CHOCOLATE PUDDING 34

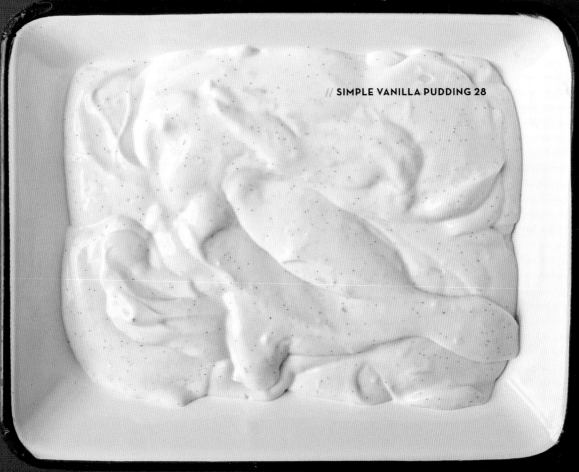

// SIMPLE VANILLA PUDDING 28

RICH VANILLA PUDDING

Last year, I went looking for my perfect vanilla pudding. There are times for Simple Vanilla Pudding (page 28) and then there are times for rich, decadent vanilla custard—my ideal.

What does my perfect pudding taste like? It tastes purely of vanilla and cream; it is speckled with real vanilla seeds. It is smooth and silky, without a whisper of a lump. Rich, not too sweet. It has to be good warm as well as cold. In the pursuit of this pudding, I tried many, many variations. In some, the egg was more assertive than the vanilla. Some were too rich, especially after chilling, with unpleasant butterfat coating the tongue. Others were grainy from cooked egg whites. But I finally worked my way to the perfect pudding I had tasted in my mind.

This is a true vanilla pudding, thickened with egg yolks and fragrant with vanilla. It mounds up on your spoon like a thick cloud. This is serious pudding; rich enough for dessert after Sunday supper, but still light and silky.

MAKES 4 CUPS (960 ML) OR EIGHT SERVINGS.

- ¼ **cup (32 g) cornstarch**
- ½ **teaspoon salt**
- 1½ **cups (360 ml) cream**
- 3 **large egg yolks**
- 2 **cups (480 ml) whole milk**
- 6 **tablespoons (75 g) sugar**
- 1 **vanilla bean, or 2 teaspoons pure vanilla extract**

Make a cornstarch and egg yolk slurry: Put the cornstarch and salt in a medium bowl and whisk out any lumps. Slowly whisk in the cream, making sure there are no lumps. Whisk in the egg yolks. It is important that this mixture be as smooth as you can make it. (To be really sure, reach into the bowl and gently rub out any lumps between your fingers.)

Warm the milk and open a vanilla bean: Warm the milk with the sugar over medium heat in a 3-quart (2.8-L) saucepan. Meanwhile, if you are using the vanilla bean, open and scrape it out into the pan (see Note). Whisk the mixture so the vanilla seeds are incorporated into the liquid. (It should look speckled, like milk after an Oreo has been dunked in it repeatedly!) When the vanilla bean has been scraped out, drop the entire pod into the milk as well.

Warm until bubbles form around the edge of the milk and the entire surface begins to vibrate. Remove the vanilla bean and discard it. Turn off the heat.

Temper the slurry: Pour 1 cup (240 ml) of the hot milk into the bowl with the slurry. Whisk vigorously to combine. The mixture should come together smoothly, with no lumps. If you see any, add a little more liquid and whisk them out. Pour the combined mixture back into the pot slowly, counting to 10 as you do and whisking vigorously.

Thicken the pudding: Turn the heat back on to medium. As the milk comes to a simmer, stir constantly but slowly with a wooden spoon, scraping the bottom of the pan evenly so that the milk doesn't scorch or form a thick skin on the bottom of the pan. In 2 to 5 minutes, the custard will come to a boil, with large bubbles that slowly pop up to the surface. Boil, whisking constantly, for 2 minutes.

Flavor the pudding: Turn off the heat. (If you didn't use a vanilla bean, stir in the vanilla extract now.)

Chill the pudding: Immediately pour the hot custard into a shallow container. Place plastic wrap or buttered wax paper directly on the surface of the pudding (if you don't like pudding skin). Put a lid on the dish and refrigerate it. This pudding is firm enough to be eaten warm after 30 minutes or so in the refrigerator.

EASY RECIPE ADAPTATION
rich vanilla cream filling for cakes or pastries

This vanilla pudding—thickened with both cornstarch and eggs—has close to the classic proportions of pastry cream, which the French call *crème pâtissière*. It is thick enough to be a filling in a cake or pastry. If you would like to use this pudding as a filling for a cake, add two additional tablespoons of cornstarch and three additional egg yolks. This will result in a thicker concoction, which, when chilled, you can use to fill cakes or pipe into éclairs.

NOTE // To scrape a vanilla bean, lay the bean flat on a cutting board and use a small, sharp paring knife to make a slit down its entire length. Splay it open with your fingers over the pot of warming milk, and run the tip of a spoon (or the knife, carefully) down the length of the bean to thoroughly scrape out the paste of tiny seeds inside.

THE VERY FIRST PUDDING: CHICKEN PUDDING!

Where did pudding come from? What was the very first pudding supped off a spoon? We know that rice and grain puddings were eaten thousands of years ago, but the history of the smooth, creamy thing we call pudding today began in medieval times with a dish called **blancmange**—and this "pudding" had a very unexpected ingredient: chicken!

"Chicken pudding" was a dish made for kings and wealthy nobility. It was a thick, creamy stew or wobbly shaped mold made from finely pureed chicken, almonds, sugar, and milk. The earliest blancmange recipes were not altogether sweet or savory, since salt was an expensive luxury, and both sugar and savory spices like pepper were used together for flavor. Eventually cornstarch and gelatin replaced chicken as a thickener, and blancmange became less of a festive dish for the upper class and more of a recommended nourishment for invalids.

I have actually eaten blancmange, medieval-style—it is a little sweet, a little savory, redolent of chicken, like a fine, rich pâté. It is creamy, in a rough sort of way, and white, too—both highly valued qualities in medieval cuisine. It was strange to my palate, but deliciously unexpected, with an aroma of spices that made me believe I truly was eating the very first pudding.

SIMPLE CHOCOLATE PUDDING

I admit to you that I am not a true chocolate aficionado. I don't dream of dark chocolate bars, or hoard shiny squares of bitter chocolate to nibble in secret. Cocoa has my heart. When I crave chocolate, it has milk in it—like the sweet, milky hot cocoa my mother poured from a saucepan after we came in from the snow. This pudding is really a cocoa pudding, made with a heap of powdered cocoa and not too much sugar. It's chocolate at its gentlest, easy to make and much better than a pudding cup.

If you want something darker, try the Rich Chocolate Custard (page 36) or the Deepest Chocolate Mousse (page 127).

MAKES 4 CUPS (960 ML) OR EIGHT SERVINGS. GLUTEN-FREE.

- ¼ cup (20 g) unsweetened cocoa powder
- ¼ cup (32 g) cornstarch
- ½ teaspoon salt
- 4 cups (960 ml) whole milk, divided (see Note)
- 6 tablespoons (75 g) sugar
- 1 teaspoon pure vanilla extract

NOTE // The results of this recipe are still acceptable (although the pudding is thinner) with 2 percent milk. I do not recommend using skim or 1 percent.

Make a cornstarch slurry: Put the cocoa powder, cornstarch, and salt in a medium bowl and whisk to make sure there are no lumps. Slowly whisk in 1 cup (240 ml) of the milk, making sure there are no lumps. The cocoa will be slow to incorporate; just keep whisking until the mixture is smooth and foamy on top. (To be really sure that the mixture is smooth, dip your fingers into the milk, gently stirring and rubbing out any lumps.)

Warm the milk: Whisk the remaining 3 cups (720 ml) milk with the sugar, over medium heat in a 2-quart (2-L) or larger saucepan. (Resist the urge to turn it to high, as this puts you at a greater risk of scorching the milk. The higher the heat, the more attentive you should be.)

As the milk comes to a simmer, stir frequently but slowly with a wooden spoon, scraping the bottom of the pan evenly so that the milk doesn't scorch or form a thick skin on the bottom of the pan. When the surface of the milk begins to quiver and vibrate, turn off the heat.

Temper the slurry: Pour 1 cup (240 ml) of the hot milk into the bowl with the slurry. Whisk vigorously to combine. The mixture should come together smoothly, with no lumps. If you see any, add a little more liquid and whisk them out. Pour the tempered slurry back into the pan slowly, counting to 10 as you do and whisking vigorously.

Thicken the pudding: Turn the heat back on to medium. In 2 to 5 minutes, the custard will come to a boil, with large bubbles that slowly pop up to the surface. Boil for 2 minutes, whisking constantly. The pudding should thicken rapidly.

Flavor the pudding: Turn off the heat and gently stir in the vanilla.

Chill the pudding: Immediately pour the hot pudding into a shallow container. Place plastic wrap or buttered wax paper directly on the surface of the pudding (if you don't like pudding skin). Let it cool slightly in the refrigerator before eating, or chill until completely cold.

Would you like to re-create the pleasure of those chocolate-vanilla pudding cups you ate as a kid? Here's how to make your own. Just make a batch of the Simple Chocolate Pudding (page 28) and a half-batch of Simple Vanilla Pudding (page 28). Chill the puddings thoroughly and whip each of them.

Divide the chocolate pudding among eight ⅓-pint (250-ml) jars, spreading ¼ cup (60 ml) chocolate pudding in the bottom of each jar. Add an equal amount of the vanilla pudding, then top with a final layer of chocolate pudding. Top each jar with a dollop of whipped cream, if desired. Serve immediately, or refrigerate, covered, for up to 3 days.

EASY FLAVOR VARIATIONS
garden mint and cocoa pudding

Before making the pudding, warm the milk almost to boiling, then add 1 cup fresh, chopped mint leaves. Turn off the heat and put the milk with the leaves in the fridge for at least 1 hour or up to 24 hours. Strain out the leaves, then proceed as directed. The mint-infused milk will give the pudding a gentle herbal flavor that I prefer to the sharpness of peppermint extract.

peppermint cocoa pudding

Substitute 1 teaspoon peppermint extract for the vanilla extract.

spicy mexican chocolate pudding

Whisk in ½ teaspoon cinnamon and ¼ teaspoon chipotle powder in addition to the vanilla extract.

Cocoa powder is made from cacao beans that have had most of their fatty cocoa butter removed. These cocoa solids are crushed into crunchy bits (cacao nibs—a great pudding topping!) or powdered into cocoa.

You may have seen recipes calling for "Dutch-processed" cocoa—what's the difference between this and regular cocoa? Natural cocoa powder has that rich chocolate flavor, but also a lot of acids—think about how tangy chocolate can be on your tongue. Dutch-processing removes some of this acid content, leaving the chocolate mellow, with less of an aftertaste. Dutch-processed cocoa is usually darker and browner than reddish regular cocoa powder.

You can use any kind of cocoa in these pudding recipes (unlike in baking, where cocoa's acid levels need to be balanced out with the right kind of leavener). Experiment with tangier, redder cocoa powder and with dark cocoa powder—which can be almost Oreo-esque in its blackness. I personally really enjoy Hershey's Special Dark cocoa powder, which is a mix of natural and Dutched cocoa powders.

RICH CHOCOLATE CUSTARD

If you love rich chocolate puddings, try this one. The thick dark-chocolate creaminess is so intense that when you drag a spoon through a bowlful, you'll leave a smooth trough. Top it with a dollop of whipped cream to balance the richness. You can also adjust the darkness of the pudding by using a darker or lighter chocolate, as you prefer.

MAKES 4 CUPS (960 ML)
OR EIGHT SERVINGS.
GLUTEN-FREE.

- 6 ounces (170 g) semisweet or bittersweet chocolate, finely chopped
- 3 tablespoons cornstarch
- ¼ teaspoon salt
- 1 cup (240 ml) cream
- 3 large egg yolks
- ½ cup (100 g) sugar
- 2 cups (480 ml) whole milk
- 1 teaspoon pure vanilla extract

Prepare the chocolate: Place the chopped chocolate in a medium heatproof bowl.

Make a cornstarch and egg slurry: Put the cornstarch and salt together in a medium bowl and whisk to make sure there are no lumps. Slowly whisk in the cream, making sure there are no lumps. (To be really sure, reach into the bowl and gently rub out any lumps between your fingers.) Whisk in the egg yolks.

Warm the milk: In a 3-quart (2.8-L) saucepan over medium heat, whisk the sugar into the milk. Warm for 3 to 5 minutes, until the sugar dissolves, bubbles form around the edges, and the entire surface of the milk begins to quiver. Turn off the heat.

Temper the slurry: Pour 1 cup (240 ml) of the hot milk into the bowl with the slurry, whisking constantly. The mixture should come together smoothly, with no lumps. If you see any, add a little more liquid and whisk them out. Pour it back into the pan, counting to 10 and whisking constantly as you pour.

Thicken the pudding: Turn the heat back on to medium and bring the mixture to a simmer, whisking frequently and vigorously, working all the angles of the pot and scraping the bottom. Continue whisking for about 5 minutes, until the custard becomes very thick and starts to boil, with large bubbles that slowly pop up to the surface. Boil for 2 minutes, whisking constantly.

Flavor the pudding: Turn off the heat and stir in the vanilla extract. Stir the chocolate into the pudding and let sit for 2 to 3 minutes. Whisk gently until the pudding is smooth and glossy and has fully absorbed the chocolate.

Chill the pudding: Immediately pour the hot pudding into a shallow container. Place plastic wrap or buttered wax paper directly on the surface of the pudding (if you don't like pudding skin). Cover and refrigerate.

EASY FLAVOR VARIATION
rich mocha pudding

To make a coffee-spiked chocolate pudding, substitute ½ cup freshly brewed coffee for ½ cup of the milk. Add 3 teaspoons espresso powder (*not* ground espresso beans; see Sources, page 213) to the cornstarch mixture.

CLASSIC CRÈME ANGLAISE

Crème anglaise is a classic rich custard with a thin consistency. It's most often used for pouring over other desserts, like pound cake or even ice cream. I include it here because it makes an indulgent topping for panna cotta (see chapter 3), and also because a bit of warm crème anglaise poured over fresh fruit like strawberries or peaches is one of the nicest desserts on a summer evening.

MAKES 2 CUPS (480 ML) OR 8 SERVINGS. GLUTEN-FREE.

- 1 **cup (240 ml) cream**
- 1 **cup (240 ml) whole milk, divided**
- ⅓ **cup (65 g) sugar**
- 1 **vanilla bean, or 2 teaspoons pure vanilla extract**
- 6 **large egg yolks**

Warm and flavor the dairy: Whisk together the cream and half of the milk in a 2-quart (2-L) saucepan; stir in the sugar.

If you're using the vanilla bean, scrape it and add the seeds to the pan (see Note, page 33). Whisk the mixture so the vanilla seeds are incorporated into the liquid. (It should look speckled, like milk after an Oreo has been dunked in it repeatedly!) When the vanilla bean has been scraped out, drop the entire bean into the pan as well. Warm the mixture just until bubbles appear around the edges and the sugar is completely dissolved, then turn off the heat.

Make an egg yolk slurry: Whisk the egg yolks for at least 1 minute in a medium bowl, then whisk in the remaining milk.

Temper the egg yolks: Add about ½ cup (120 ml) of the warmed dairy to the slurry and whisk to combine. Slowly pour this mixture back into the pan and whisk to combine. (If you didn't use a vanilla bean, stir in the vanilla extract now.)

Thicken the pudding: Turn the heat back on to medium-low and cook the custard for 5 minutes, or until it thickens slightly and leaves a shiny and opaque coating on the back of a spoon. Test by drawing your finger through this coating; if it leaves a distinct line, the custard is done.

Chill the pudding: Strain the custard through a fine-mesh sieve into a shallow container and discard the vanilla bean. Refrigerate for 30 minutes, if you're planning to serve it lukewarm, or up to 3 days. Crème anglaise can be gently rewarmed in a saucepan over low heat.

BUTTERSCOTCH PUDDING

What is butterscotch? And what's the difference between butterscotch and caramel? They both involve cooked sugar, but caramel is made with white sugar, and butterscotch with brown. The toasty sweet flavor of butterscotch comes from cooking brown sugar with butter until it begins to caramelize. The result is probably my favorite pudding of all: rich, creamy, and nutty, with the toasted sweetness of dark sugar and butter.

MAKES 4 CUPS (960 ML)
OR EIGHT SERVINGS.
GLUTEN-FREE.

- ¼ cup (32 g) cornstarch
- ½ teaspoon salt
- 2½ cups (600 ml) whole milk
- 3 large egg yolks, beaten
- 4 tablespoons (56 g) unsalted butter
- ¾ cup (165 g) tightly packed light brown sugar
- 1 cup (240 ml) cream
- 1 teaspoon pure vanilla extract
- 1 tablespoon bourbon (optional)

Make a cornstarch and egg yolk slurry: Put the cornstarch in a large bowl with the salt. Slowly whisk in the milk until you have a smooth mixture. (To be really sure, reach into the bowl and gently rub out any lumps between your fingers.) Whisk in the egg yolks and set aside.

Make the butterscotch: Place the butter in a deep 3-quart (2.8-L) or larger saucepan set over medium-high heat, and when it has melted completely, stir in the sugar. The mixture will look clumpy and grainy like wet sand, but as the sugar melts, it will smooth out. Cook the sugar, whisking frequently, until it emulsifies with the butter and becomes one molten substance. Don't walk away; keep an eye on it! The mixture will also change color slightly and darken. From the time you've added the sugar, this will take about 5 minutes total. As the sugar cooks, it will eventually begin to smoke. Watch carefully for that first stream of smoke—as soon as you see it, turn off the heat.

Warm the cream: Carefully pour the cream into the pan of sugar. Sugar will bubble up violently and hot steam will rise from the pan. Whisk vigorously as the cream is poured in. This may cause the hot sugar to clump up and seize at first, but keep whisking; it will dissolve in the cream. When the cream is fully incorporated, turn the heat back on to medium, whisking constantly.

Temper the slurry and thicken the pudding: Pour about half of the hot cream into the slurry and whisk vigorously to combine. When it is perfectly smooth, pour the mixture back into the saucepan slowly, counting to 10 as you do and whisking constantly. Bring the pudding back to a boil, whisking constantly and vigorously working all the angles of the pot and scraping the bottom. It will take 2 to 5 minutes for the custard to come to a boil, with large bubbles that slowly pop up to the surface. Boil for 2 minutes, still whisking constantly.

Flavor the pudding: Turn off the heat and stir in the vanilla extract and the bourbon, if using.

Chill the pudding: Immediately pour the hot pudding into a shallow dish or divide it into individual dishes. Place plastic wrap or buttered wax paper directly on the surface and refrigerate for 1 hour, or until set.

DOUBLE COCONUT CREAM PUDDING
WITH COCONUT BRITTLE

This pudding is milky and fresh, tasting of real coconut, and topped with a fabulous crispy coconut brittle that tastes like the inside of a Butterfinger candy bar.

For this pudding, look for coconut milk that has not been blended or homogenized with added stabilizers. I prefer the Thai brand Chaokoh, which can be found in almost any Asian supermarket.

MAKES 4 CUPS (960 ML)
OR EIGHT SERVINGS.
GLUTEN-FREE.

- **2 cups (180 g) shredded sweetened coconut**
- **³/₄ cup (180 ml) cream**
- **1¹/₂ cups (360 ml) whole milk**
- **6 tablespoons (75 g) sugar**
- **3 tablespoons cornstarch**
- **¹/₂ teaspoon salt**
- **1 (13.5-ounce / 400-ml) can coconut milk**
- **1 large egg**
- **1 large egg yolk**
- **¹/₂ teaspoon pure vanilla extract**
- **1 teaspoon dark rum (optional)**

Toast the coconut: Put the coconut in a 3-quart (2.8-L) saucepan over medium heat. Cook, stirring very frequently, for about 3 minutes, or until the coconut has turned light tan. It will give off a lot of steam and dry out slightly. Watch carefully, as it will quickly turn from toasted to burnt.

Flavor the cream and milk: Add the cream and milk to the pan, and whisk in the sugar. Bring to a simmer and turn off the heat. Steep for 15 minutes, then strain out and discard the coconut and return the liquid to the pan.

Make a cornstarch and egg slurry: Put the cornstarch and salt in a medium bowl and whisk out any lumps. Slowly whisk in the coconut milk, making sure there are no lumps. Whisk in the egg and egg yolk. It is important that this mixture be as smooth as you can make it. (To be really sure, reach into the bowl and gently rub out any lumps between your fingers.)

Warm the dairy: Return the strained cream mixture to low heat. Warm it just until the surface quivers. Turn off the heat.

Temper the slurry: Pour 1 cup (240 ml) of the cream mixture into the slurry and whisk vigorously to combine. The mixture should come together smoothly, with no lumps. If you see any, add a little more liquid and whisk them out. Slowly pour the tempered slurry back into the pan, counting to 10 as you do and whisking continuously and vigorously.

Thicken the pudding: Turn the heat back on to medium. Work all the angles of the pot, and scrape the bottom as you whisk. It will take 2 to 5 minutes to bring the custard to a boil, with large bubbles that slowly pop up to the surface. Boil, whisking constantly, for 2 minutes.

Flavor the pudding: Turn off the heat. Stir in the vanilla extract and rum, if using.

Chill the pudding: Immediately pour the pudding into a shallow container, and place plastic wrap or buttered wax paper directly on the surface of the pudding (if you don't like pudding skin). Refrigerate. Eat warm or chilled. Serve with toasted coconut brittle (recipe follows).

TOASTED COCONUT BRITTLE

This stuff tastes far better than it has a right to—after all, it's little more than cooked sugar mixed with toasted unsweetened coconut. I increase the ratio of coconut to sugar, so it tastes more of coconut than of brittle, and then chop it into fine crumbles. Eaten by the spoonful, it may just remind you of the inside of a Butterfinger candy bar.

MAKES ABOUT 2 CUPS OR EIGHT SERVINGS (480 ML). GLUTEN-FREE.

- ½ tablespoon (7 g) unsalted butter, plus more for the bowl and spoon
- 2 cups (160 g) shredded unsweetened coconut
- ½ teaspoon kosher salt
- ¼ teaspoon ground ginger
- ½ cup (100 g) sugar
- 2 tablespoons warm water
- 1 tablespoon light corn syrup

Lightly butter a large metal mixing bowl and silicone or rubber mixing spoon.

Melt the butter in a 3-quart (2.8-L) saucepan over medium-high heat until it foams up. Add the coconut and cook, stirring constantly, for about 3 minutes, or until it is evenly toasted to a golden brown color. Turn off the heat and toss the coconut with the salt and ginger. Pour the coconut into the buttered bowl. Rinse out the pan and wipe it completely clean and dry.

Add the sugar to the saucepan and stir in the warm water and the corn syrup. Turn the heat back on to medium-high and whisk the mixture to dissolve the sugar. When it comes to a rolling boil, stop stirring. Boil for 5 to 8 minutes, or until the sugar begins to turn light brown. Keep a close eye on it; it will go from light brown to burnt very quickly. Gently swirl the pan as the sugar changes color. It will turn dark amber and begin to smoke. As soon as you see that first wisp of smoke, turn off the heat and carefully pour the syrup in a slow stream into the bowl with the coconut.

Stir to completely mix the syrup with the coconut. Let cool for 15 minutes, stirring occasionally to break up big clumps as the sugar hardens. When the mixture has mostly cooled, use a big metal spoon, bench scraper, or sturdy pastry blender to chop the brittle into fine crumbs. (You can also run it through a food processor.)

Store these fine crumbs of coconut brittle in an airtight container for up to 2 weeks. (It won't go bad, but eventually moisture will leak in and cause it to lose its snap.)

Serve sprinkled over Double Coconut Cream Pudding (opposite page), or any other pudding. It's good on almost everything.

PUMPKIN SPICE PUDDING
WITH HONEY CARAMEL SAUCE

This pudding takes pumpkin puree and the traditional spices of autumn desserts—cinnamon, ginger, and cloves—and brings them together in a creamy pudding. It's lighter than the eggy filling of a pumpkin pie, and very good topped with caramel sauce, whipped cream, and a dusting of fresh nutmeg.

MAKES 4 CUPS (960 ML)
OR EIGHT SERVINGS.
GLUTEN-FREE.

- ¼ cup (32 g) cornstarch
- ½ teaspoon salt
- 1 cup (240 ml) cream
- 3 large egg yolks
- ½ tablespoon (7 g) unsalted butter
- ½ cup (120 ml) canned pumpkin puree (do not use pumpkin pie filling)
- 1 teaspoon cinnamon (see Note)
- 1 teaspoon ground ginger
- ¼ teaspoon nutmeg
- ¼ teaspoon ground cloves
- ⅛ teaspoon allspice
- 2 cups (480 ml) whole milk
- ¼ cup (50 g) granulated sugar
- ¼ cup (55 g) packed dark brown sugar
- 1 teaspoon pure vanilla extract

Make a cornstarch and egg yolk slurry: Put the cornstarch and salt in a medium bowl and whisk out any lumps. Slowly whisk in the cream, making sure there are no lumps. Whisk in the egg yolks. It is important that this mixture be as smooth as you can make it. (To be really sure, reach into the bowl and gently rub out any lumps between your fingers.)

Flavor and warm the milk: Heat the butter in a 3-quart (2.8-L) saucepan over medium heat. Tilt the pan to help the butter coat the bottom. Drop in the pumpkin puree and sauté over medium heat for 2 to 3 minutes, cooking the puree just enough to remove the raw taste. Stir in the cinnamon, ginger, nutmeg, cloves, and allspice. Slowly whisk in the milk and add both the sugars.

Warm over medium heat until bubbles form around the edge of the milk and the entire surface begins to quiver. Turn off the heat.

Temper the slurry: Pour 1 cup (240 ml) of the hot milk into the slurry. Whisk vigorously to combine. The mixture should come together smoothly, with no lumps. If you see any, add a little more liquid and whisk them out. Pour the combined mixture back into the pot slowly, counting to 10 as you do and whisking vigorously.

Thicken the pudding: Turn the heat back on to medium, whisking continuously and vigorously. Work all the angles of the pot, and scrape the bottom. It will take 2 to 5 minutes to bring the custard to a boil, with large bubbles that slowly pop up to the surface. Boil, whisking constantly, for 2 minutes. Turn off the heat. Stir in the vanilla extract.

Chill the pudding: Immediately pour the custard into a shallow container. Place plastic wrap or buttered wax paper directly on the surface of the pudding (if you don't like pudding skin). Refrigerate for 1 hour, if eating warm, or 3 hours, if you wish to eat it fully chilled.

Serve with honey caramel sauce (recipe follows), whipped cream, and freshly grated nutmeg.

NOTE // If you have pumpkin pie spice in your spice cabinet, you can substitute 2½ teaspoons of that for the cinnamon, ginger, nutmeg, cloves, and allspice.

HONEY CARAMEL SAUCE

Honey flavors a sweet, fragrant spin on the usual caramel sauce. The honey also helps the sugar dissolve without seizing or crystallizing. You can use light corn syrup instead.

MAKES ABOUT 1 CUP (240 ML). GLUTEN-FREE.

- ³/₄ cup (150 g) sugar
- 1 tablespoon honey
- ³/₄ cup (180 ml) cream
- 1 teaspoon pure vanilla extract
- ¹/₄ teaspoon salt

Whisk the sugar, ¹/₄ cup (60 ml) water, and the honey together in a heavy 2-quart (2-L) saucepan. Turn the heat on to high and bring the mixture to a full rolling boil, stirring until the sugar dissolves. This will take 3 to 5 minutes. Lower the heat to medium and let it boil vigorously, without stirring. After 5 minutes, check for hints of darkening color in the syrup (apart from the color of the honey). If you don't detect any, continue boiling until you do. This will take anywhere from 5 to 10 minutes of vigorous boiling, depending on the strength of your stove burner and the weight of your pan. Keep a close eye on things. (If you have a candy thermometer, you can make this easier by using it. Heat the sugar syrup to 350°F / 175°C or slightly higher. Don't go beyond 375°F / 190°C.)

You will begin to see streaks of a medium-brown color form around the edges. When this happens, take the pan by the handle and gently swirl it to help the sugar combine. Watch carefully: Once you see the first color change, the syrup can turn from amber-colored to burnt very quickly.

When the syrup is completely amber-colored, add the cream in a slow, thin stream and use a long-handled whisk to carefully whisk it together with the hot sugar syrup. Be cautious, as the syrup will bubble up furiously. Don't be concerned if the sugar hardens into a lump at first; keep whisking vigorously and it will melt and combine smoothly. When the sugar and cream are completely mixed, bring them back to a simmer and cook for 3 minutes.

Remove from the heat, stir in the vanilla and salt, and let cool. This sauce can be refrigerated in a closed container for up to 3 months.

MALTED MILK PUDDING
WITH HOT FUDGE SAUCE

Malted milk powder was invented in the late nineteenth century as a nutritious, shelf-stable milk product for infants and invalids. It's made from barley that has been sprouted, dried, and mixed with powdered milk. It's naturally sweet, and the distinctive malty flavor became popular for many uses: It was added to milk shakes and other soda shop drinks, and people stirred it into cocoa for a comforting evening beverage. Personally, I love that malted flavor; it's old-fashioned and a little special, something to set a simple vanilla pudding apart. This pudding tastes extra-milky with the sweet, toasted flavor of malt.

Unlike most of the puddings in this book, this one is not gluten-free, as malted milk powder is made with wheat and barley.

**MAKES 4 CUPS (960 ML)
OR EIGHT SERVINGS.**

¼ cup (32 g) cornstarch

5 tablespoons (35 g) malted milk powder

½ teaspoon salt

1 cup (240 ml) cream

2 large egg yolks

2½ cups (600 ml) whole milk

6 tablespoons (75 g) sugar

1 teaspoon pure vanilla extract

Make a cornstarch and egg yolk slurry: Put the cornstarch, malt, and salt in a medium bowl, and whisk out any lumps. Slowly whisk in the cream, making sure there are no lumps. Whisk in the egg yolks. It is important that this mixture be as smooth as you can make it. (To be really sure, reach into the bowl and gently rub out any lumps between your fingers.)

Warm the milk: Whisk the milk with the sugar over medium heat in a 3-quart (2.8-L) saucepan. When bubbles form around the edge of the milk and the entire surface begins to quiver, turn off the heat.

Temper the slurry: Pour 1 cup (240 ml) of the hot milk into the slurry. Whisk vigorously to combine. The mixture should come together smoothly, with no lumps. If you see any, add a little more liquid and whisk them out. Pour the tempered slurry back into the pan slowly, counting to 10 as you do and whisking constantly and vigorously.

Thicken the pudding: Turn the heat back on to medium. Whisk constantly, working all the angles of the pan, and scrape the bottom. It will take 2 to 5 minutes to bring the custard to a boil, with large bubbles that slowly pop up to the surface. Boil, whisking constantly, for 2 minutes.

Flavor the pudding: Turn off the heat. Stir in the vanilla.

Chill the pudding: Immediately pour the custard into a shallow container. Place plastic wrap or buttered wax paper directly on the surface of the pudding (if you don't like pudding skin). Refrigerate.

This pudding is firm enough to be eaten warm after only 30 minutes or so in the refrigerator. Drizzle it with Old-fashioned Hot Fudge Sauce (recipe follows) when serving.

OLD-FASHIONED HOT FUDGE SAUCE

Many fudge sauce recipes are actually variations on chocolate ganache, made from cream and melted chocolate. Not this one; it's a true old-fashioned fudge sauce, made from bitter chocolate and butter. It is perfectly glossy and not too sweet, and it lasts for up to two weeks in the refrigerator.

MAKES ABOUT 1 CUP (240 ML). GLUTEN-FREE.

- 2 tablespoons (28 g) unsalted butter
- 2 ounces (55 g) unsweetened chocolate, finely chopped
- 3/4 cup (150 g) sugar
- 1/3 cup (75 ml) boiling water
- 2 tablespoons light corn syrup
- 1/4 teaspoon salt

Melt the butter and chocolate in a small saucepan over low heat, stirring frequently. When the chocolate is melted, stir in the sugar, water, corn syrup, and salt. Bring to a boil, stirring to make sure the sugar dissolves, then stop stirring and let the mixture boil for 6 minutes, or until it has thickened and become glossy.

This will keep in the fridge for about 2 weeks and can be frozen for several months. Reheat over low heat on the stove, or on low power in the microwave, stopping frequently to stir.

DORIE GREENSPAN ON GREAT CRÈME BRÛLÉE

I asked Dorie Greenspan, author of *Around My French Table* and many other books on delicious French baking and sweets, about what makes a great crème brûlée, and why it is such an enduring classic. "The most defining and luscious characteristic of crème brûlée," she said, "is the temperature and flavor contrast—sweet to bittersweet, and cool and creamy to hot caramel. It only gets better as you eat it, too—the first and second bites set you up to appreciate the whole dessert. It's more fun if the sugar top isn't an even thickness, because then every bite is different, a different ratio of sugar to cream. Each mouthful can be a surprise."

NO-BAKE CRÈME BRÛLÉE

Traditionally, crème brûlée is a baked custard: egg yolks and cream poured into ramekins, set in a water bath, and baked in the oven. I find the whole process a little fussy and difficult. If you want that effortlessly smooth, rich, restaurant-style crème brûlée, then this no-bake stovetop method is the way to go.

MAKES EIGHT ½-CUP (120-ML) SERVINGS. GLUTEN-FREE.

- 2 **tablespoons cornstarch**
- ¼ **teaspoon salt**
- 2½ **cups (600 ml) cream**
- 8 **large egg yolks**
- 1 **cup (240 ml) whole milk**
- 6 **tablespoons (75 g) sugar**
- 1 **vanilla bean, or 2 teaspoons pure vanilla extract**

  Fine turbinado sugar, for brûléeing

Make a cornstarch and egg yolk slurry: Put the cornstarch and salt in a medium bowl, and whisk out any lumps. Slowly whisk in the cream, making sure there are no lumps. Whisk in the egg yolks. It is important that this mixture be as smooth as you can make it.

Warm and flavor the milk: Whisk the milk with the sugar over medium heat in a 3-quart (2.8-L) saucepan. If you're using the vanilla bean, scrape it and add the seeds to the pan (see Note, page 33). Whisk the mixture so the seeds are incorporated into the liquid. (It should look speckled, like milk after an Oreo has been dunked in it repeatedly!) When the vanilla bean has been scraped out, drop the entire pod into the pan as well.

Warm until bubbles form around the edge of the milk and the entire surface begins to quiver. Remove the vanilla bean and discard it. Turn off the heat.

Temper the slurry: Pour all of the milk mixture into the slurry. Whisk vigorously to combine. The mixture should come together smoothly, with no lumps. Pour the mixture back into the pan.

Thicken the pudding: Turn the heat back on to medium and bring to a simmer, whisking constantly and vigorously. Work all the angles of the pot, and scrape the bottom. It will take 2 to 5 minutes to bring the custard to a boil, with large bubbles that slowly pop up to the surface. Boil, whisking constantly, for 2 minutes. Turn off the heat. (If you didn't use a vanilla bean, stir in the vanilla extract now.)

Strain and chill the pudding: Pass the custard through a fine-mesh strainer. Pour it into eight ½-cup (120-ml) ovenproof ramekins and refrigerate. Do not cover them; in this case, you want a thin, dry skin to form on top. Chill the puddings for at least 4 hours, or overnight.

Brûlée the pudding! Lightly sprinkle the surface of each pudding with an even layer of turbinado sugar. Shake the ramekins from side to side to even out the layer. Use a kitchen torch to caramelize the sugar. Let sit 5 minutes before serving so the sugar layer can cool and harden.

Alternate method: Make sure your ramekins are broiler-safe. Move a rack up to the highest position and heat your broiler. Broil the ramekins for 3 to 7 minutes, until the sugar is evenly melted and browned. Keep a close watch and turn the ramekins once or twice to help them brown evenly.

BANANA PUDDING SUPREME
WITH CARAMELIZED BANANAS

What's more old-school than banana pudding? Bowlful of childhood nostalgia coming right up! The only problem is that the banana pudding of our youth got its taste through artificial flavor granules and yellow dye. This has the creamy texture of beloved banana pudding but is infused with natural flavors.

MAKES 4 CUPS (960 ML)
OR EIGHT SERVINGS.
GLUTEN-FREE.

- 2 **small ripe bananas, about 12 ounces (340 g)**
- ⅓ **cup (65 g) sugar**
- 2½ **cups (600 ml) whole milk**
- 3 **tablespoons cornstarch**
- ½ **teaspoon salt**
- ¾ **cup (180 ml) cream**
- 2 **large egg yolks**
- 1 **teaspoon pure vanilla extract**

NOTE // This pudding lacks that fake yellow color that telegraphs *banana* before you even take a bite. If you want a bit of yellow color, stir in ⅛ teaspoon turmeric powder with the vanilla.

Flavor and warm the milk: In a 3-quart (2.8-L) saucepan, thoroughly mash together the bananas and sugar. Pour in the milk. Warm over medium heat almost to boiling (the surface of the milk should quiver and vibrate). Turn off the heat.

Blend and rewarm the milk: Purée the banana-milk mixture in a food processor or blender. Pour it back into the pan and warm it for 3 to 5 minutes over medium heat, until bubbles form around the edges and the center of the milk is vibrating. Turn off the heat.

Make a cornstarch and egg yolk slurry: Put the cornstarch and salt in a medium bowl. Slowly whisk in the cream, making sure there are no lumps. Whisk in the egg yolks. It is important that this mixture be as smooth as you can make it. (To be really sure, reach into the bowl and gently rub out any lumps.)

Temper the slurry: Pour a ladleful of the hot milk into the bowl with the slurry. Whisk vigorously to combine. The mixture should come together smoothly, with no lumps. If you see any, add a little more liquid and whisk them out. Pour this mixture back into the pan slowly, counting to 10 as you do and whisking constantly and vigorously.

Thicken the pudding: Turn the heat back on to medium. Work all the angles of the pan, and scrape the bottom. It will take 2 to 5 minutes to bring the custard to a boil, with large bubbles that slowly pop up to the surface. Boil, whisking constantly, for 2 minutes. Turn off the heat and stir in the vanilla.

Chill the pudding: Immediately pour the custard into a shallow container. Place plastic wrap or buttered wax paper directly on the surface to cover it, and refrigerate for 2 hours, or until fully chilled. Serve with caramelized bananas (recipe follows).

EASY FLAVOR VARIATION
banana cream pudding

For a milder, more subtle banana flavor, with no specks of the fruit and with more emphasis on the cream, you can strain out the mashed bananas before heating the milk.

CARAMELIZED BANANAS

These bananas add a sweet, caramelized topping to pudding. They are very good on banana, vanilla, or peanut butter pudding—or spread over a dish of chocolate panna cotta.

MAKES EIGHT SERVINGS.
GLUTEN-FREE.

- 2 **tablespoons (28 g) unsalted butter**
- ¼ **cup (55 g) packed brown sugar**
- ¼ **teaspoon salt**
- 4 **small bananas, ripe yet firm**

Melt the butter over medium-high heat in a deep skillet. When it foams up, stir in the sugar and salt. The mixture will clump up at first, but it will melt quickly and form a bubbling, liquid mass.

Meanwhile, peel and slice the bananas into coins about ½ inch (12 mm) thick and put them in a large bowl. When the sugar has completely melted, pour it into the bowl with the bananas and toss to coat. Turn the heat to high and transfer the sugar-coated bananas into the pan. Cook on high for about 2 minutes, flipping and stirring the bananas after the first minute. Serve hot.

TOASTED COCONUT

Nutty, fragrant toasted coconut is a tasty topping for nearly any pudding, but I particularly like it on pineapple pudding. I recommend using unsweetened coconut flakes instead of sweetened, since the pudding is sweet enough on its own and the coconut should balance that sweetness. But if all you have are sweetened coconut flakes, it's perfectly fine to use them. Most recipes toast the coconut in the oven, but I prefer using a saucepan on the stovetop, as it is easier to toast it precisely to your liking and there's less risk of burning it.

MAKES 1 CUP (240 ML).
GLUTEN-FREE.

- ½ **tablespoon (7 g) unsalted butter**
- 1 **cup (60 g) unsweetened coconut flakes**

Heat the butter in a 3-quart (2.8-L) saucepan or deep skillet over medium heat. When it foams up, pour in the coconut and cook, stirring frequently, until it is deep golden brown and smells toasted. Take the pan off the heat and completely cool the topping in the pan, stirring occasionally. Store it in a sealed container for up to 5 days.

PINEAPPLE PUDDING
WITH TOASTED COCONUT

This pudding will bring to mind the sweet summer picnic salads of family reunions and potlucks past—an ambrosial mix of marshmallows, coconut, and canned pineapple. It's sweet and a little salty and, unlike most of the puddings in this chapter, it has *texture*. Little nubs of pineapple swim in a creamy custard, and the whole thing is topped with delicate strands of nutty toasted coconut. It's like a tiki bar in a bowl.

MAKES 4 CUPS (960 ML) OR EIGHT SERVINGS. GLUTEN-FREE.

2½ cups (600 ml) whole milk

8 ounces (225 g) dried sweetened pineapple chunks, chopped

2 tablespoons cornstarch

¼ teaspoon salt

½ cup (120 ml) cream

1 large egg yolk

Warm and flavor the milk: Warm the milk in a 3-quart (2.8-L) saucepan over medium heat until it is almost to boiling (the surface should quiver and vibrate). Turn off the heat and stir in the pineapple. Set aside to steep for 15 minutes. Pour the mixture into a blender and blend carefully until only very fine bits of pineapple remain. (You can also use a stick blender, but it will be harder to incorporate the pineapple completely.) Pour the mixture back into the saucepan and rewarm it over medium heat until bubbles form around the edge of the milk and the surface begins to vibrate. Turn off the heat.

Make a cornstarch and egg yolk slurry: Put the cornstarch and salt in a medium bowl and whisk out any lumps. Slowly whisk in the cream, making sure there are no lumps. Whisk in the egg yolk. It is important that this mixture be as smooth as you can make it. (To be really sure, reach into the bowl and gently rub out any lumps between your fingers.)

Temper the slurry: Pour a ladleful of the hot milk into the bowl with the slurry. Whisk vigorously to combine. The mixture should come together smoothly, with no lumps (you will see small nubs of pineapple). If you see lumps, add a little more liquid and whisk them out. Pour the tempered slurry back into the pan slowly, counting to 10 as you do and whisking constantly and vigorously.

Thicken the pudding: Turn the heat back on to medium. Whisk constantly and vigorously, working all the angles of the pot and scraping the bottom. It will take 2 to 5 minutes to bring the custard to a boil, with large bubbles that slowly pop up to the surface. Boil, whisking constantly, for 2 minutes. Turn off the heat.

Chill the pudding: Immediately pour the custard into a shallow container. Place plastic wrap or buttered wax paper directly on the surface to cover it, and refrigerate for 2 hours to chill thoroughly. Serve with a sprinkle of toasted coconut (recipe on facing page) or Toasted Coconut Brittle (page 41).

LEMON AND SOUR CREAM CUSTARD

Given a choice, I'll pick a lemon dessert nearly every time. This tangy, fresh lemon pudding is based in part on an ice cream I created for my wedding reception. I made quarts of fresh lemon ice cream, sweet but with a puckered edge, and this pudding borrows that flavor of fresh, clean lemons in sweet cream—a taste that for me will always mean sunshine and joy.

MAKES 4 CUPS (960 ML)
OR EIGHT SERVINGS.
GLUTEN-FREE.

- 3 tablespoons cornstarch
- ½ teaspoon salt
- ¾ cup (180 ml) cream, divided
- 2 ounces (55 g) cream cheese, very soft
- 2 large egg yolks
- 2 cups (480 ml) whole milk
- ½ cup (100 g) sugar
- 2 lemons, zested and juiced (about 6 tablespoons / 90 ml juice)
- 1 cup (240 ml) full-fat sour cream

Make a cornstarch and cream slurry: Put the cornstarch and salt in a medium bowl and whisk out any lumps. Slowly pour in ½ cup (120 ml) of the cream, whisking constantly until there are no lumps. (To be really sure, reach into the bowl and gently rub out any lumps between your fingers.)

In a separate medium bowl, whisk the cheese vigorously until it looks whipped and soft. Slowly add the remaining ¼ cup (60 ml) cream, whisking until the mixture is smooth. Pour in the slurry and whisk until smooth. Whisk in the egg yolks.

Warm and flavor the milk: Place a 3-quart (2.8-L) saucepan on the stove and whisk the milk, sugar, and lemon zest together in the pan. Turn the heat on to medium. (Resist the urge to turn the heat to high, as this puts you at a greater risk of scorching the milk. The higher the heat, the more attentive you should be.)

As the milk comes to a simmer, stir constantly but slowly with a wooden spoon, scraping the bottom of the pan evenly so that the milk doesn't scorch or form a thick skin on the bottom of the pan. When the surface of the milk begins to quiver and vibrate, turn off the heat.

Temper the slurry: Pour 1 cup (240 ml) of the hot milk into the bowl with the slurry. Whisk them together. The mixture should come together smoothly, with no lumps. Pour the tempered slurry slowly back into the pan, counting to 10 as you do and whisking vigorously to combine them.

Thicken the pudding: Turn the heat back on to medium. Bring the pudding to a boil; this will take 2 to 5 minutes. When large bubbles slowly pop up to the surface, reduce the heat and let the pudding simmer for 2 full minutes. Continue to whisk vigorously. Turn off the heat.

Chill the pudding: Immediately pour the hot pudding into a shallow container. (If you notice lumps in the pudding, you can pour it through a fine-mesh strainer to make it smoother.) Gently fold in the sour cream. Place plastic wrap or buttered wax paper directly on the surface of the pudding to cover it. Put a lid on the dish and refrigerate.

Flavor the pudding: Chill the pudding for 1 hour, then stir in the lemon juice. Return it to the fridge and chill it completely. It is best refrigerated overnight and eaten when very cold.

CARAMEL PUDDING WITH BUTTERED APPLES

As I write this, the weather has just turned to fall, and leaves are wetly plastered to the sidewalks. The brightest, cheeriest thing in the kitchen right now is a red apple, picked from a local orchard. Its warm color promises something sweet and tasty—as does this pudding, richly flavored with caramelized sugar and butter, with tender bites of warm spiced apples folded in.

MAKES 4 CUPS (960 ML)
OR EIGHT SERVINGS.
GLUTEN-FREE.

for the pudding

¼ cup (32 g) cornstarch

½ teaspoon salt

½ teaspoon ground ginger

2½ cups (600 ml) whole milk

3 large egg yolks, beaten

2 tablespoons (28 g) unsalted butter

½ cup (100 g) sugar

¾ cup (180 ml) cream

1 teaspoon pure vanilla extract

for the apples

2 medium, firm apples, such as Rome or Fuji, about 1 pound (455 g)

2 tablespoons (28 g) unsalted butter

¼ cup (55 g) packed dark brown sugar

1 teaspoon cinnamon

¼ teaspoon nutmeg

¼ teaspoon ground cloves

Make a cornstarch and egg yolk slurry: Put the cornstarch in a large bowl with the salt and ginger. Slowly whisk in the milk until you have a smooth mixture. (To be really sure, reach into the bowl and rub out any lumps between your fingers.) Whisk in the egg yolks and set aside.

Make the caramel: Melt the butter with the sugar in a deep 3-quart (2.8-L) or larger saucepan over medium heat. The mixture will look clumpy and grainy at first, but it will smooth out. Turn the heat down so the sugar is simmering in a gooey mass on the bottom of the pan. Cook over low heat for 5 minutes. Watch carefully; if the sugar begins to smoke, turn down the heat. Cook until the sugar begins to turn a golden color, swirling the pan as it darkens. Take it off the heat. Slowly pour in the cream, whisking constantly. Be careful, as the cream and hot sugar will bubble up violently. Whisk until the sugar is completely dissolved.

Temper the slurry: Pour most of the hot liquid into the slurry and whisk to combine. When it is perfectly smooth, pour the mixture back into the saucepan.

Thicken the pudding: Turn the heat on to medium and bring the pudding back up to a simmer. Whisk vigorously, working all the angles of the pot and scraping the bottom. It will take 2 to 5 minutes to bring the custard to a boil, with large bubbles that slowly pop up to the surface. Boil for 2 full minutes, whisking constantly. Turn off the heat and stir in the vanilla.

Chill the pudding: Immediately pour the hot pudding into a shallow container. Place plastic wrap or buttered wax paper directly on the surface of the pudding and refrigerate while you prepare the apples.

Make the apple mix-in: Peel and core the apples. Cut them into slices ¼ inch (6 mm) thick, then cut those slices into pieces about 1 inch (2.5 cm) across. Melt the butter in a skillet over medium heat and stir in the sugar, cinnamon, nutmeg, and cloves. Cook until the sugar is molten, then stir in the apples until they are completely coated. Cook for 10 minutes, or until they are tender but not yet mushy.

Fold the apples into the pudding: Let the apples cool for a few minutes, then stir them into the pudding. Serve the pudding warm, or chill it completely.

SCARLET ROSE AND BERRY PUDDING
WITH WHIPPED CREAM

This unusual, dairy-free pudding is nevertheless creamy and delicious—and it has the most luscious color! It's based on a traditional Danish pudding made in summertime when currants, raspberries, and strawberries are at their peak, and the color is bright red or hot pink, depending on the mix of fruit. It's also similar to a British dessert called flummery, a stewed pudding of fruit and cornstarch. While fresh June strawberries are the ultimate base for this pudding, it can be made any time of year using frozen berries. Taste the mixture as you add sugar; if your berries are fresh and sweet, you may not need all the sugar called for.

MAKES 4 CUPS (960 ML) OR EIGHT SERVINGS. GLUTEN-FREE. DAIRY-FREE.

- ¼ cup (32 g) cornstarch
- ¼ teaspoon salt
- 2 large egg yolks
- 10 ounces (280 g) strawberries or mixed berries, fresh or frozen (thawed)
- 10 ounces (280 g) raspberries, fresh or frozen (thawed)
- 6 tablespoons (75 g) sugar
- 1 lemon, juiced (about 3 tablespoons / 45 ml juice)
- 1 teaspoon rosewater (see Note)
- Whipped cream (see page 167), to serve

NOTE // Rosewater is a distillation of rose petals, a highly fragrant by-product of the perfume industry. Look for it in the baking aisle or at gourmet shops (see Sources, page 213). Be sure you are buying food-grade rosewater.

Make a cornstarch and egg yolk slurry: Put the cornstarch and salt in a medium bowl and whisk out any lumps. Slowly pour in 1 cup (240 ml) water, whisking constantly. Whisk in the egg yolks. (To be really sure, reach into the bowl and gently rub out any lumps between your fingers.)

Blend and warm the berries: Puree the strawberries and raspberries with the sugar and lemon juice in a blender until smooth and liquefied. Pour through a fine-mesh sieve into a 3-quart (2.8-L) saucepan. Turn the heat on to high and bring the fruit mixture to a simmer, stirring frequently. Turn off the heat.

Temper the slurry: Pour 1 cup (240 ml) of the hot fruit into the bowl with the slurry. Whisk them together. Pour the tempered slurry slowly back into the pan, counting to 10 as you do and whisking vigorously.

Thicken the pudding: Turn the heat back on to medium. Bring the pudding to a full boil, whisking frequently; this will take 2 to 5 minutes. Large bubbles will rise up very slowly, making a noise like *gloop* or *plop*.

Simmer for 2 minutes, whisking frequently. Turn off the heat and whisk in the rosewater.

Chill the pudding: Immediately pour the hot pudding into a shallow container. (If you notice lumps, you can pour the pudding through a fine-mesh sieve to make it smoother.) Place plastic wrap or buttered wax paper directly on the surface of the pudding to cover it. Put a lid on the dish and refrigerate. Chill for 2 hours, or until completely cold, before eating. Best eaten within 3 days.

Serve in dessert cups with a dollop of whipped cream on top.

ROASTED PISTACHIO PUDDING

When I was a kid, I loved pistachio pudding with all my heart. I remember ripping open the little packet of green dust and pouring it into a bowl of milk, then whipping up magical pistachio pudding—pale mint-green, with crystalline flecks of dried pistachio.

    This pudding evokes nostalgia for that pistachio pudding, but it is so much better. Unlike the unreal color of the boxed pudding, it's pale yellow-green, like real pistachios, which are not pure green but shot through with brown and violet. It has the smooth richness of real cream and egg yolks, and the nutty finish of roasted pistachio nutmeats. It's pistachio pudding all grown up, but still a little magical.

MAKES 4 CUPS (960 ML) OR EIGHT SERVINGS. GLUTEN-FREE.

- 3 **cups (300 g) shell-on, roasted pistachios (see Note)**
- ⅔ **cup (130 g) sugar, divided**
- 2½ **cups (600 ml) whole milk, divided**
- 1 **cup (240 ml) cream**
- 3 **tablespoons cornstarch**
- ¼ **teaspoon salt**
- 2 **large egg yolks**
- ½ **teaspoon pure vanilla extract**
- ½ **teaspoon almond extract**

Prepare the pistachios: Shell the pistachios. You should have approximately 1⅓ cups (315 ml) pistachio nutmeats. Finely chop or grind ⅓ cup (75 ml) of the nutmeats and set aside. Meanwhile, put a kettle of water on to boil.

Place the remaining pistachios in a ceramic or metal bowl. Pour the boiling water over them so they are completely covered. Let them steep for 15 minutes, then drain. Spread them out on a paper towel and use a second paper towel to rub them vigorously. Pick the nutmeats away from the papery skins, peeling still-attached skin away as necessary. (This is tedious but essential for flavor and for color; the skins will give a bitter taste to the pudding.)

Create a pistachio paste: Place the skinless pistachios in the work bowl of a food processor. Add half of the sugar and 2 tablespoons water and blend until you have a fine, wet paste.

Flavor the dairy: Put this paste in a 2-quart (2-L) saucepan and add 2 cups (480 ml) of the milk, the cream, and the remaining sugar. Bring to a simmer over medium-high heat, stirring frequently. Turn off the heat.

Make a cornstarch and egg yolk slurry: Put the cornstarch and salt in a medium bowl, and whisk out any lumps. Slowly whisk in the remaining ½ cup (120 ml) milk, making sure there are no lumps. Whisk in the egg yolks. It is important that this mixture be as smooth as you can make it. (To be really sure, reach into the bowl and gently rub out any lumps between your fingers.)

Warm the dairy: Strain the pistachio-milk mixture and discard the pistachio solids. Pour the liquid back into the saucepan and warm over medium heat until the surface of the milk begins to vibrate.

Temper the slurry: Pour 1 cup (240 ml) of the hot milk into the bowl with the slurry and whisk vigorously to combine. They should come together smoothly, with no lumps. If you see any, add a little more liquid and whisk them out. Pour the mixture slowly back into the pot, counting to 10 as you do and whisking vigorously.

RECIPE CONTINUES

NOTE // While I enjoy the convenience of preshelled pistachio nutmeats, which I can find in my grocer's bulk foods section, I've found that it is best to buy pistachios in the shell and shell them myself. Why? The taste is significantly better. Preshelled roasted pistachios often taste bitter and a little stale, and some are downright moldy. The shells protect their freshness. As long as you're going to the trouble of making delicious pudding, you may as well make sure it tastes as good as possible!

Thicken the pudding: Turn the heat back on to medium. It will take 2 to 5 minutes to bring the custard to a boil, with large bubbles that slowly pop up to the surface. Boil, whisking constantly, for 2 minutes.

Flavor the pudding: Turn off the heat and stir in the vanilla and almond extracts. Stir in the reserved chopped pistachios.

Chill the pudding: Immediately pour the custard into a shallow container. Place plastic wrap or buttered wax paper directly on the surface to cover it, and refrigerate. This pudding is firm enough to be eaten warm after about 1 hour in the refrigerator.

For a Greener Pistachio Pudding: This pudding will not be the bright artificial green of instant Jell-O pistachio pudding. It's a pale green-yellow. If you would like to increase the green quotient, use raw pistachios instead of roasted, and make sure to remove every last bit of skin in the blanching step. It still won't give you a shocking bright-green pudding, but it will be much closer. (Still finish the pudding, though, with those roasted chopped pistachios.)

DARK CHOCOLATE GANACHE

Ganache is the simplest sort of chocolate sauce: good chocolate, cream, and a pat of butter for gloss and shine.

MAKES 1 CUP (240 ML).
GLUTEN-FREE.

- 4 **ounces (115 g) semisweet or bittersweet chocolate, finely chopped**
- ½ **cup (120 ml) cream**
- 1 **tablespoon (14 g) unsalted butter**

Place the chocolate in a small metal, glass, or ceramic bowl. Heat the cream in a small saucepan over medium heat until bubbles form around the edges and the surface begins to quiver. Pour the hot cream over the chocolate. Let it sit for a couple of minutes, then add the butter and whisk the mixture until it is evenly smooth and glossy.

This can be made up to 3 days ahead of time and refrigerated. Warm it over low heat or in the microwave and stir before drizzling it over the pudding.

PEANUT BUTTER AND HONEY PUDDING
WITH DARK CHOCOLATE GANACHE

What's more crowd-pleasing than peanut butter and chocolate? Think Reese's Peanut Butter Cups, buckeye balls, Moose Tracks ice cream. This honeyed peanut butter pudding is simple and not too sweet, but finish it off with a drizzle of rich chocolate ganache, and it becomes something extra special.

MAKES 4 CUPS (960 ML)
OR EIGHT SERVINGS.
GLUTEN-FREE.

- 3 tablespoons cornstarch
- 1/4 teaspoon salt
- 3/4 cup (180 ml) cream
- 2 large egg yolks
- 2 cups (480 ml) whole milk
- 1/4 cup (60 ml) honey
- 1/4 cup (55 g) packed dark brown sugar
- 3/4 cup (180 ml) natural creamy salted peanut butter, well stirred (see Note)
- 1 teaspoon pure vanilla extract

NOTE // I prefer to use natural salted peanut butter, such as Smucker's Natural Creamy Peanut Butter, with no additional sugar or processed additives. Just peanuts and salt! Stir the peanut butter well to make sure any separated oils are fully reincorporated.

Make a cornstarch and egg yolk slurry: Put the cornstarch and salt in a medium bowl, and whisk out any lumps. Slowly whisk in the cream, making sure there are no lumps. Whisk in the egg yolks. It is important that this mixture be as smooth as you can make it. (To be really sure, reach into the bowl and gently rub out any lumps between your fingers.)

Warm and sweeten the milk: Whisk the milk, honey, and sugar in a 2-quart (2-L) saucepan over medium heat until bubbles form around the edge of the milk and the entire surface begins to quiver. Turn off the heat.

Temper the slurry: Pour 1 cup (240 ml) of the hot milk into the bowl with the slurry and whisk vigorously to combine. They should come together smoothly, with no lumps. If you see any lumps, add a little more liquid and whisk them out. Pour the tempered slurry back into the pan slowly, counting to 10 as you do and whisking vigorously.

Thicken the pudding: Turn the heat back on to medium. It will take 2 to 5 minutes to bring the custard to a boil, with large bubbles that slowly pop up to the surface. Boil, whisking constantly, for 2 minutes. Turn off the heat.

Flavor the pudding: Whisk in the peanut butter and the vanilla.

Chill the pudding: Immediately pour the custard into a shallow container. Place plastic wrap or buttered wax paper directly on the surface to cover it, and refrigerate. This pudding is firm enough to be eaten warm after 30 minutes or so in the refrigerator. Serve with a drizzle of Dark Chocolate Ganache (page 58).

NUTELLA PUDDING
WITH HAZELNUT BRITTLE

I encountered Nutella the summer after graduating college. I was in Italy, and my youth hostel served small, precious packets of this hazelnut-flavored chocolate spread with our morning bread. I looked forward to its sticky-smooth richness every morning. What was once a European delicacy is now easily found in America, right next to the peanut butter and jelly—lucky us! If I had to choose one crowd favorite from this chapter, Nutella pudding would win, hands down. All my testers raved about this pudding, with its rich chocolate-and-hazelnut creaminess. The hazelnut brittle puts it over the top: dark and a little bitter, with the nutty crunch of whole hazelnuts.

MAKES 4 CUPS (960 ML)
OR EIGHT SERVINGS.
GLUTEN-FREE.

- 3 tablespoons cornstarch
- ½ teaspoon salt
- 1 cup (240 ml) cream
- 2 large egg yolks
- 2 cups (480 ml) whole milk
- ¼ cup (50 g) sugar
- ¾ cup Nutella (or other brand of chocolate-hazelnut spread)
- ½ teaspoon pure vanilla extract

Make a cornstarch and egg yolk slurry: Put the cornstarch and salt in a medium bowl, and whisk out any lumps. Slowly whisk in the cream, making sure there are no lumps. Whisk in the egg yolks. It is important that this mixture be as smooth as you can make it. (To be really sure, reach into the bowl and gently rub out any lumps between your fingers.)

Warm the milk: Whisk the milk and sugar over medium heat in a 3-quart (2.8-L) saucepan until bubbles form around the edge of the milk and the entire surface begins to quiver. Turn off the heat.

Temper the cornstarch: Pour 1 cup (240 ml) of the hot milk into the bowl with the slurry and whisk vigorously to combine. They should come together smoothly, with no lumps. If you see any, add a little more liquid and whisk them out. Pour the tempered slurry back into the pan slowly, counting to 10 as you do and whisking vigorously.

Thicken the pudding: Turn the heat back on to medium. It will take 2 to 5 minutes to bring the custard to a boil, with large bubbles that slowly pop up to the surface. Boil, whisking constantly, for 2 minutes. Turn off the heat.

Flavor the pudding: Put the Nutella in a bowl and ladle in about 1 cup (240 ml) of the hot pudding. Whisk until smooth, then add the Nutella mixture back to the pan. Whisk until thoroughly combined, add the vanilla, and stir.

Chill the pudding: Immediately pour the custard into a shallow container. Place plastic wrap or buttered wax paper directly on the surface to cover it, and refrigerate. This pudding is firm enough to be eaten warm after 30 minutes or so in the refrigerator. Serve with hazelnut brittle (recipe follows) sprinkled over the top.

HAZELNUT BRITTLE

This is a crunchy brittle that makes thick shards of crushed hazelnuts and sugar, perfect for garnishing a glass of warm Nutella pudding.

MAKES ABOUT 1 CUP (240 ML). GLUTEN-FREE.

- ½ **cup (100 g) sugar**
- 2 **tablespoons (28 g) unsalted butter**
- 1 **tablespoon light corn syrup**
- ⅛ **teaspoon baking soda**
- 1 **cup (115 g) roughly chopped hazelnuts, toasted**
- 1 **teaspoon kosher salt**

Lightly butter a large baking sheet and a silicone spatula or spoon and set them aside.

In a medium saucepan, bring the sugar, 2 tablespoons water, the butter, and corn syrup to a vigorous rolling boil over medium-high heat. Cook for 5 to 7 minutes without stirring, watching carefully. When the sugar turns a yellowish color, swirl the pan gently. The sugar will rapidly turn from pale yellow to light tan to a dark amber color. When the sugar gives off a thin stream of smoke, remove it from the heat and immediately stir in the baking soda; take care—the mixture will bubble up violently. Stir in the hazelnuts and salt.

Immediately scrape the nut mixture out onto the prepared baking sheet and spread it ¼ to ½ inch (6 to 12 mm) thick. Cool for at least 30 minutes. When the brittle is cool and hard, use a large knife to break it into fine shards. Store in an airtight container.

HOW TO MAKE PUDDING POPS

For me, Pudding Pops are a cherished treat from childhood. I don't remember ever having them at home, but my grandmother kept her freezer stocked with vanilla Pudding Pops and Fudgsicles. I have fond memories of raiding her freezer for these exotic treats—richer than Popsicles, more fun to eat than ice cream.

You can easily make these frozen treats in your own kitchen with homemade pudding. Here are a few tips.

» Once you have frozen a cornstarch pudding, you can't *unfreeze* it! So only freeze pudding if you know you want to eat it frozen.

» One batch of the regular puddings in this chapter will make twelve to sixteen pops. To make them, pour slightly warm or room-temperature pudding into ice-pop molds. I especially like the Norpro Ice Pop Maker, which makes ten pops at a time, and the Tovolo Groovy Ice Pop Molds, which make six.

» The best puddings for pops will be ones with egg yolks, like Rich Vanilla Pudding (page 32) and Rich Chocolate Custard (page 36).

» **Other puddings to try in pop form:** Banana Pudding Supreme (page 48), Peanut Butter and Honey Pudding (page 59), and Nutella Pudding (page 60).

MAPLE-BOURBON BUDINO
WITH SPICED PECANS

Maple and bourbon were meant to go together, with maple's sweet fragrance and bourbon's vanilla smoothness. They pair especially well in this intensely rich and sweet budino, which mounds up on the spoon like creamy maple syrup. It's best eaten warm.

MAKES 2 CUPS (480 ML) OR EIGHT SERVINGS. GLUTEN-FREE.

- ¼ cup (55 g) packed dark brown sugar
- ¼ cup (60 ml) Grade B maple syrup (see Note)
- 1 cup (240 ml) cream
- 2 tablespoons cornstarch
- ½ teaspoon kosher salt
- ¾ cup (180 ml) whole milk
- 3 large egg yolks
- 1 teaspoon pure vanilla extract
- 2 tablespoons bourbon

Warm and sweeten the cream: Bring the sugar and maple syrup to a boil over medium heat in a 3-quart (2.8-L) saucepan. Turn the heat to low and simmer for 10 minutes, or until the mixture is reduced by about half. Whisk in the cream and heat until the surface begins to quiver. Turn off the heat.

Make a cornstarch and egg yolk slurry: Meanwhile, whisk the cornstarch and salt together in a medium bowl. Slowly whisk in the milk, making sure there are no lumps. Whisk in the egg yolks. It is important that this mixture be as smooth as you can make it. (To be really sure, reach into the bowl and gently rub out any lumps between your fingers.)

Temper the slurry: Pour 1 cup (240 ml) of the hot cream into the bowl with the slurry and whisk vigorously to combine. They should come together smoothly, with no lumps. If you see any, add a little more liquid and whisk them out. Pour the tempered slurry back into the pan slowly, counting to 10 as you do and whisking vigorously.

Thicken the pudding: Turn the heat back on to medium. Bring the mixture to a simmer, whisking constantly and vigorously, working all the angles of the pot and scraping the bottom. It will take 2 to 5 minutes for the custard to come to a boil, with large bubbles that slowly pop up to the surface. Boil, whisking constantly, for 2 minutes. Turn off the heat. Stir in the vanilla and bourbon.

Chill the pudding: Immediately pour the custard into a shallow container. Place plastic wrap or buttered wax paper directly on the surface to cover it, and refrigerate. This recipe is best served warm—almost immediately, or after 30 minutes in the refrigerator. Serve it with a spoonful of spiced maple pecans (recipe follows) scattered on top.

NOTE // Grade B maple syrup is known as "cooking grade" syrup. Much darker and stronger in flavor than Grade A, it is available at Whole Foods and other gourmet-food purveyors (see Sources, page 213). Be sure to use real maple syrup, not the imitation varieties found on some supermarket shelves.

SPICED MAPLE PECANS

These lightly toasted spiced pecans are just piquant enough to balance the sweet richness of the Maple-Bourbon Budino.

MAKES 1 CUP (240 ML).
GLUTEN-FREE.

- 1 **cup (110 g) roughly chopped pecans**
- ¼ **teaspoon cinnamon**
- ⅛ **teaspoon ground ginger**
- ⅛ **teaspoon chipotle powder**
- 1 **tablespoon (14 g) unsalted butter**
- 2 **tablespoons Grade B maple syrup (see Note, facing page)**
- ½ **teaspoon kosher salt**

Butter a baking sheet and have it ready. Heat a large skillet over medium-high heat and add the pecans. Cook for about 3 minutes, stirring frequently, until they smell nutty and toasted. Add the spices and cook for 10 seconds, stirring. Add the butter and maple syrup and stir until melted, then bring to a simmer. As soon as the liquid bubbles down into a thick glaze, remove the pan from the heat. Stir in the salt. Turn out onto the baking sheet. Store in an airtight container for up to 1 week.

CHEESECAKE BUDINO
WITH BRANDIED CHERRY SAUCE

Cheesecake in a cup: That's this pudding. The cheesecake flavor is initially mild, but it intensifies after a night in the refrigerator. For best flavor, I suggest you make it two days before you intend to serve it.

MAKES 2 CUPS (480 ML) OR EIGHT SERVINGS. GLUTEN-FREE.

- 2 tablespoons cornstarch
- ½ teaspoon kosher salt
- 1 cup (240 ml) cream, divided
- 4 ounces (115 g) cream cheese, softened at room temperature for at least 1 hour
- 1 large egg yolk
- ¼ cup (50 g) sugar
- 1 cup (240 ml) whole milk
- 1 teaspoon pure vanilla extract

Make a cornstarch and egg yolk slurry: Put the cornstarch and salt in a medium bowl and whisk out any lumps. Slowly whisk in half of the cream until there are no lumps in the mixture. (To be really sure that the mixture is smooth, reach into the bowl and gently rub out any lumps between your fingers.)

In a separate medium bowl, whisk the cream cheese vigorously until it looks whipped and very smooth. Slowly whisk in the remaining cream until the mixture is smooth. Pour in the cornstarch and cream mixture and whisk until smooth. Whisk in the egg yolk.

Warm the milk: Whisk the sugar and milk together in a 2-quart (2-L) or larger saucepan. Turn the heat on to medium. (Resist the urge to turn the heat to high, as this puts you at a greater risk of scorching the milk. The higher the heat, the more attentive you should be.)

As the milk comes to a simmer, stir constantly but slowly with a wooden spoon, scraping the bottom of the pan evenly so that the milk doesn't scorch or form a thick skin on the bottom of the pan. When the surface of the milk begins to quiver and vibrate, turn off the heat.

Temper the slurry: Pour 1 cup (240 ml) of the hot milk into the bowl with the slurry. Whisk them together, then pour the tempered slurry slowly back into the pan, counting to 10 as you do and whisking vigorously.

Thicken the pudding: Turn the heat back on to medium and bring the pudding to a boil. Whisk constantly and vigorously, working all the angles of the pot and scraping the bottom. It will take 2 to 5 minutes for the custard to boil, with large bubbles that slowly surface.

Lower the heat and let it boil for 2 full minutes, whisking constantly. Turn off the heat and whisk in the vanilla.

Chill the pudding: Immediately pour the hot pudding into a shallow container. (If you notice lumps in the pudding, you can pour it through a mesh strainer to make it smoother.) Place plastic wrap or buttered wax paper directly on the surface of the pudding to cover it. Put a lid on the dish and chill it completely. This is good served 4 hours after cooking, but the flavor will be most intense after 2 nights. Serve it cold, with Brandied Cherry Sauce (page 66) on top.

BRANDIED CHERRY SAUCE

Here's a grown-up version of the scarlet, viscous cherry sauce traditionally draped over classic cheesecake. This sauce is darker, richer, and boozier—and it tastes like real cherries.

¼ cup (50 g) sugar

1 teaspoon cornstarch

Pinch salt

1 lemon, juiced (about 3 tablespoons)

¼ cup (60 ml) brandy

1 pound (455 g) pitted fresh sweet cherries (or thawed frozen cherries), halved

1 teaspoon pure vanilla extract

Whisk together the sugar, cornstarch, and salt in a 2-quart (2-L) saucepan. Whisk in ¼ cup (60 ml) water and the lemon juice until the mixture is smooth. Whisk in the brandy, and stir in the cherries. Cook over medium heat until the mixture comes to a boil. Simmer for 3 minutes, or until the sauce thickens and the cherries are warmed through. Turn off the heat and stir in the vanilla. Serve immediately, or refrigerate for up to 1 week.

CHOCOLATE-BUTTERSCOTCH BUDINO

Another extra-rich budino, this calls for cooking butterscotch until dark and nearly smoky, then adding chocolate. If you are in the mood for something warm, sweet, and hearty enough to satisfy your last craving, this is your pudding. It's best served warm or at room temperature.

MAKES 2 CUPS (480 ML)
OR EIGHT SERVINGS.
GLUTEN-FREE.

- 1 tablespoon cornstarch
- ½ teaspoon kosher salt
- ½ cup (120 ml) whole milk
- 2 large egg yolks
- ⅓ cup (75 g) packed dark brown sugar
- 1¼ cups (300 ml) cream
- 2 tablespoons (28 g) unsalted butter, cut into small pieces
- 2 ounces (55 g) bittersweet chocolate, finely chopped
- 1 tablespoon brandy or rum (optional)

Make a cornstarch and egg yolk slurry: Put the cornstarch and salt in a medium bowl, and whisk out any lumps. Slowly whisk in the milk, making sure there are no lumps. Whisk in the egg yolks. It is important that this mixture be as smooth as you can make it. (To be really sure, reach into the bowl and gently rub out any lumps between your fingers.)

Make the butterscotch: Whisk the sugar together with ⅔ cup (158 ml) water in a 3-quart (2.8-L) or larger saucepan and bring to a boil over medium-high heat, whisking frequently to help dissolve the sugar. When the mixture comes to a boil, stop stirring and boil for 5 to 7 minutes, until the sugar's color changes and darkens. As the sugar darkens, gently swirl the pan. As soon as you see the first hint of smoke coming up from the sugar, pour in the cream, whisking constantly. Be careful: The sugar will bubble and steam furiously. Whisk out any lumps and bring back to a simmer.

Temper the slurry: Pour about half of the hot cream mixture into the bowl with the slurry. Whisk vigorously to combine. They should come together smoothly, with no lumps. If you see any, add a little more liquid and whisk them out. Pour the tempered slurry back into the pan slowly, counting to 10 as you do and whisking vigorously.

Thicken the pudding: Turn the heat back on to medium. It will take 2 to 5 minutes to bring the custard to a boil, with large bubbles that slowly pop up to the surface. Boil, whisking constantly, for 2 minutes. Turn off the heat.

Flavor the pudding: Whisk in the butter, chocolate, and liquor, if using.

Chill the pudding: Immediately pour the custard into a shallow container. Place plastic wrap or buttered wax paper directly on the surface to cover it, and refrigerate. This pudding is firm enough to be eaten warm after 30 minutes or so in the refrigerator.

CHAI-WHITE CHOCOLATE BUDINO

This pudding has a milky sweetness and the fragrant spiciness of chai (spiced tea). It's silky smooth—the smoothest pudding in this whole chapter. Serve it in elegant porcelain cups, with a cup of tea.

MAKES 2 CUPS (480 ML)
OR EIGHT SERVINGS.
GLUTEN-FREE.

¾ cup (180 ml) whole milk

1½ cups (360 ml) cream, divided

2 tablespoons sugar

4 chai tea bags

1 tablespoon cornstarch

¼ teaspoon salt

2 large egg yolks

½ cup (about 3 ounces / 85 g) white chocolate discs, such as 31% Cacao White Chocolate Wafers from E. Guittard, roughly chopped

Warm and flavor the milk: Whisk the milk, ½ cup (120 ml) of the cream, and the sugar in a medium saucepan, and drop in the tea bags. Warm over medium heat until bubbles form around the edges and the surface of the milk begins to vibrate. Turn off the heat and let steep for 5 minutes. Discard the tea bags.

Make a cornstarch and egg yolk slurry: Put the cornstarch and salt in a medium bowl, and whisk out any lumps. Slowly whisk in the remaining 1 cup (240 ml) cream, making sure there are no lumps. Whisk in the egg yolks. It is important that this mixture be as smooth as you can make it. (To be really sure, reach into the bowl and gently rub out any lumps between your fingers.)

Temper the slurry: Pour the hot chai-infused milk into the bowl with the slurry. Whisk vigorously to combine. They should come together smoothly, with no lumps. If you see any, add a little more liquid and whisk them out. Pour the tempered slurry back into the pot slowly, counting to 10 as you do and whisking vigorously.

Thicken the pudding: Turn the heat back on to medium. It will take 2 to 5 minutes to bring the custard to a boil, with large bubbles that slowly pop up to the surface. Boil, whisking constantly, for 2 minutes. Turn off the heat.

Flavor the pudding: Stir in the chocolate until it is completely melted.

Chill the pudding: Immediately pour the custard into a shallow container. Place plastic wrap or buttered wax paper directly on the surface to cover it, and refrigerate. This pudding is firm enough to be eaten warm after 30 minutes or so in the refrigerator.

RICE, TAPIOCA & WHOLE-GRAIN PUDDINGS

Rice, tapioca, and whole-grain puddings are an entirely different breed from the more delicate custards and puddings in this book. We call them puddings, but really they tend to be more like sweet porridges, running the gamut from rich and creamy rice custards to earthy, barely sweetened cooked grains that would be perfectly acceptable for breakfast.

RICE PUDDING MEMORIES

Rice pudding is perhaps the ultimate comfort food, a pudding that makes most people think instantly of their childhood home cuisine. It is a very old and venerable dish—the granddaddy of puddings. It has been eaten in Rome, England, and Asia for thousands of years. Rice pudding shows up in Shakespeare's plays and medieval European recipe books, and its popularity has hardly abated today. It is nourishing, comforting, and tender, a dish that can be filling enough for breakfast or luxurious enough for a feast.

In this chapter, I pay homage to rice pudding as the oldest, homiest, and still most popular and comforting pudding treat by talking with a few friends and writers about the rice puddings they grew up with.

GRAIN PUDDING

Rice is only the beginning of grain pudding possibilities. Whole grains are enjoying a surge of popularity and I have found that many people are interested in incorporating high-fiber, high-protein grains like quinoa, barley, and even oats into sweet puddings. Many of these can double as breakfast—they're so hearty and nourishing.

BASIC METHOD FOR A RICE OR GRAIN PUDDING

These sorts of puddings are truly simple and foolproof. The basic method goes like this: Cook rice or grains, then stir in milk, cream, or eggs, and simmer until thick and creamy.

1 **Cook the rice or grains:** Many of these recipes call for cooking the rice or grains first, before adding the dairy. You can do this on the stovetop or in a convenient electric rice cooker. Other recipes call for cooking the rice or grains directly in the milk.

2 **Add sugar and dairy:** In many cases, especially when working with rice, sugar can get in the way of liquid absorption. Once the rice grains have been fully cooked, add the sweetener and the dairy called for in the recipe.

3 **Thicken the pudding:** Once the grains are cooked and you have added the sweetener and the milk, cream, or eggs, it's time to thicken the pudding. A rice or grain pudding is thickened not only by the fat in the milk that has been cooked down, but also by the starch in the grain itself. You have a lot of flexibility in this stage—if you like thinner puddings, use a little more milk or cook it for a shorter period of time. You can also add egg yolks if you want a richer pudding; just temper 2 beaten yolks with a little of the cooked pudding, then whisk in slowly and cook until it is thick and glossy (3 to 5 minutes).

4 **Flavor the pudding:** Now that the pudding is thick, turn off the heat and stir in vanilla, salt, and any other flavorings called for in the recipe.

5 **Chill the pudding:** Pour the pudding into a container and cover it loosely. Chill until it is at the desired temperature. If the pudding gets extremely thick after chilling overnight (this is common), thin it with a little extra milk while reheating.

MILK, CREAM, AND ALTERNATIVE DAIRIES IN RICE AND GRAIN PUDDINGS

Puddings made with full-fat milk and cream are certainly more luxurious and creamy, but fat plays a less essential role in grain and rice puddings. For best results, use the dairy I call for in the recipes, but know that you can experiment with lower-fat milks and alternative dairies, too.

Some of the puddings in this chapter call for other sorts of milk, in fact—like coconut milk and almond milk. I don't recommend soy milk in cooked puddings as a general rule. I find that it tends to curdle when heated. Coconut and almond are more stable.

RICE AND GRAIN PUDDING TROUBLESHOOTING

» **The pudding got too thick!** As I've said, grain puddings are flexible. If a pudding turns out too thick, just add a little more milk or liquid to thin it down. This is especially true after chilling; some puddings will turn nearly solid in the fridge. If you want to loosen them, stir in a little more liquid before reheating.

» **The rice (or grain) never got soft!** Double-check the measurements from the recipe and make sure you used the correct ratio of liquid to rice. Also, if you are making a recipe that tells you to cover the pot, check the seal on the lid and make sure that liquid isn't escaping in the form of steam. Also double-check the variety of rice. There is a difference between brown and white, and between short-, medium-, and long-grain rice in terms of how much liquid and cooking time is needed. Stick to the variety called for in the recipe.

SERVING IDEAS

Rice and grain puddings are simple treats, and I don't dress them up too much. If you want to add a touch of elegance to these rustic puddings, serve them in a glass over fruit puree, or top with some cream or whipped crème fraîche. Nuts are especially good—chopped pistachios or cashews on quinoa or Indian rice pudding are delicious. See the recipes for more serving ideas.

MAUREEN ABOOD ON LEBANESE RICE PUDDING

Maureen Abood writes about Lebanese food and culture (find her at maureenabood.com). Here, she shares a memory of her mother's most comforting rice pudding:

"The rice pudding of my dreams comes directly from the hand of my mom, which came from her mother, and her mother before that. Our rice pudding, or *roz bi haleeb* (which translates to "rice with milk"), is made with eggs, whole milk, some cream—with a rich silkiness that is given body from rice. The indulgence is heightened with a fragrant drop of traditional Lebanese flower waters—rosewater or orange blossom water—and topped with a sprinkle of salty, crunchy, vibrant green pistachios. When I eat a spoonful of Lebanese rice pudding, I am reminded how much better it is simply to taste, and to see just how good it can be."

To make Lebanese-style rice pudding, add a drop of orange blossom water or rosewater to a pot of plain rice pudding, enriched with egg yolks, and top it with pistachios, as Maureen describes.

DORIE GREENSPAN ON RICE PUDDING, THE FAMILY PUDDING OF FRANCE

Dorie Greenspan writes delightful and beautiful books about baking and French cooking. Her latest, *Around My French Table*, shares her many years of home cooking experience in France. I asked her what she considered to be the quintessential pudding of France, expecting perhaps crème brûlée or crème caramel. But, no—it was something much humbler!

"The pudding that you see most often," said Dorie, "and the one that people have the most nostalgic memories of, is rice pudding! We had a French *au pair*, and the first thing she made when she came to live with us was rice pudding, because it made her think of home and it was good for a baby too. Simple, not expensive—you can enjoy it plain. It has warmth, as in heartwarming. We fell in love with it and made it a couple times a week, sometimes with chocolate, sometimes with raisins."

"Rice pudding is this touchstone of nostalgia for French cooks," she added. "You see it more and more now among more formal restaurants. A three-star restaurant might serve it in a Mason jar. Go to a ski resort, and it's served in a big pottery bowl. It's a family sweet, a family pudding."

STOVETOP RICE PUDDING
(WITH UNCOOKED RICE)

This is the simplest, easiest, and perhaps *best* rice pudding—plain rice cooked with milk and sweetened with a touch of sugar. The finished pudding is creamy and comforting. Raisins are optional, although personally I can't imagine this pudding without those chewy, wrinkled pops of sweetness.

MAKES 3 CUPS (720 ML) OR SIX SERVINGS. GLUTEN-FREE.

- 4 cups (960 ml) whole milk
- 2/3 cup (123 g) long-grain white rice, such as basmati (see Note)
- 1/4 teaspoon salt
- 3 to 4 tablespoons (35 to 50 g) sugar, or to taste
- 1 teaspoon pure vanilla extract
- 1/2 teaspoon cinnamon
- 1/3 cup raisins (optional)

Cook the rice: Stir together the milk and rice in a heavy, lidded 2-quart (2-L) saucepan and bring to a boil over medium-high heat, stirring constantly. Turn the heat down to low and simmer, stirring frequently to avoid scorching the milk. Cook, covered, for 20 to 25 minutes, until the rice is cooked and chewy (but not mushy) and the milk has reduced to form a soupy pudding.

Sweeten and flavor the pudding: Stir in the salt, sugar, vanilla, cinnamon, and raisins, if using, and cook for an additional 3 minutes, stirring constantly. (The pudding will look quite thin, but it will thicken considerably as it cools.)

Chill the pudding: Transfer the pudding to a container and cool for 15 minutes in the refrigerator before serving.

NOTE // Do not substitute brown rice in this recipe. For a rice pudding that starts with dry brown rice, see Gingered Brown Rice Pudding with Plum Conserve (page 82).

cinnamon-coconut rice pudding

To make a Latin American–inspired rice pudding, substitute 1 (13.5-ounce / 400-ml) can coconut milk for 1½ cups (360 ml) of the whole milk. Cook as directed above, and add 1 full teaspoon of cinnamon.

lemon rice pudding

Use a sharp vegetable peeler to pare the rind off 1 lemon in long, thin strips, leaving the bitter white pith behind. Add the peel to the milk and rice, and cook as directed above. Omit the cinnamon and vanilla. Allow the finished pudding to cool slightly, then juice the lemon and stir this juice into the rice pudding. Remove the lemon peels if desired, or leave them in the pudding to provide an extra pop of flavor.

rice pudding with dried fruits

While raisins are traditional in rice pudding, I also enjoy a more eclectic mix of dried fruit. To make a tutti-frutti rice pudding, finely chop ¼ cup (35 to 40 g) each of dried dates, dried apricots, and dried cranberries. Add ¼ cup (60 ml) each of water and rum (or, if you don't prefer to add alcohol, use a full ½ cup / 120 ml water), bring to a boil, remove from the heat, and let steep for 15 minutes. Drain the fruit and add it to a finished batch of rice pudding. Garnish the finished pudding with a handful of chopped pistachios.

torch your rice pudding!

If you have a torch lying around for crème brûlée (page 47) but want to release your pyromaniac impulses a little more frequently, then try brûléeing other sorts of puddings. I enjoy a crusty, burnt-sugar top on rice pudding in particular. Sprinkle finished rice pudding with a thin layer of turbinado sugar and torch until melted and crispy.

Alternatively, you can broil the sugar topping in the oven. Heat your broiler and move a rack up to the highest position. Make sure your pudding dish is broiler-safe. Broil the pudding for 3 to 7 minutes, until the sugar is evenly melted and browned. The time required will vary widely, depending on your oven and the distance from the broiler element. Keep a close watch and turn the dish once or twice to help the pudding brown evenly. Let it cool for 5 minutes to allow the sugar to harden.

STOVETOP RICE PUDDING
(WITH COOKED RICE)

Here's another basic rice pudding that starts with cooked white rice—a great dish for using up leftover unseasoned rice and transforming it into dessert. This pudding is similar in texture to the previous rice pudding, which starts with raw rice; this just gives you another option. Whether you start with raw or cooked rice, you can have your rice pudding, pronto.

MAKES 3 CUPS (720 ML) OR SIX SERVINGS. GLUTEN-FREE.

- 3 cups (720 ml) whole milk
- 2 cups (315 g) cooked white rice (see Note)
- 3 to 4 tablespoons (35 to 50 g) sugar, or to taste
- 1 (3-inch / 7.5-cm) cinnamon stick
- 1 teaspoon pure vanilla extract
- ¼ teaspoon salt
- ⅓ cup (48 g) raisins (optional)

Thicken the pudding: Stir together the milk, rice, sugar, and cinnamon stick in a heavy, lidded 2-quart (2-L) saucepan and bring to a boil over medium-high heat, stirring constantly. Turn the heat down to low and simmer, stirring frequently to avoid scorching the milk. Cook, covered, for 20 minutes, or until the rice has absorbed much of the milk.

Sweeten and flavor the pudding: Stir in the vanilla, salt, and raisins, if using, and cook for an additional 3 to 5 minutes. (The pudding will look quite thin, but it will thicken considerably as it cools.)

Chill the pudding: Transfer the pudding to a container and cool for 15 minutes in the refrigerator before serving.

NOTE // You may substitute cooked brown rice or another variety of rice.

HOW TO MAKE RAISINS SOFTER & JUICIER

Raisins are usually quite hard and chewy, but if you'd like to give them a little more softness and flavor, you can plump them into juicier versions of themselves with water, brandy, orange juice, or any other flavorful liquid.

To plump ½ cup (73 g) raisins, heat ½ cup (120 ml) water, or ¼ cup (60 ml) water mixed with an equal amount of brandy, rum, orange juice, apple juice, or another juice or liquor to boiling. You can do this in a 2-cup (480-ml) glass measuring cup in the microwave, or in a small saucepan on the stovetop. Add the raisins to the boiling liquid and remove from the heat. Let steep for at least 15 minutes. Drain off any excess liquid and use the raisins as directed in the recipe.

ARROZ CON TRES LECHES

This is a sweeter rice pudding that's very rich, made with not one but three kinds of milk, and egg yolks, too. It's a nod to the sweet rice pudding tradition of Latin America—plus, of course, tres leches cake.

MAKES 3 CUPS (720 ML) OR SIX SERVINGS. GLUTEN-FREE.

- 1 (12-ounce / 354-ml) can full-fat evaporated milk
- 1 cup (240 ml) whole milk
- ⅔ cup (133 g) short-grain white rice, such as arborio
- 1 (3-inch / 7.5-cm) cinnamon stick, or 1/4 teaspoon ground cinnamon
- 1 vanilla bean, or 2 teaspoons pure vanilla extract

  Zest of 1 small orange, removed in 1 long strip
- 1 (14-ounce / 397-g) can sweetened condensed milk
- 2 large egg yolks
- 2 tablespoons rum (optional)
- ¼ teaspoon salt

Flavor the pudding: Mix the evaporated milk, whole milk, and 2 cups (480 ml) water in a heavy, lidded 3-quart (2.8-L) saucepan and stir in the rice. Drop in the cinnamon stick (or cinnamon).

If you're using the vanilla bean, scrape the seeds into the pan (see Note, page 33). Whisk the mixture so the vanilla seeds are incorporated into the liquid. (It should look speckled, like milk after an Oreo has been dunked in it repeatedly!) When the vanilla bean has been scraped out, drop the pod into the milk as well. Drop the orange zest into the milk.

Cook the rice: Bring the milk to a boil over medium-high heat, then reduce to a simmer and cook, covered, for 20 to 25 minutes, stirring frequently to avoid scorching the milk, until the milk has reduced to a soupy consistency and the rice is very tender. Remove and discard the vanilla bean.

Thicken the pudding: In a separate bowl, whisk together the condensed milk, egg yolks, rum (if using), and salt. Whisk in about ½ cup (120 ml) of the hot rice pudding, then slowly beat this mixture back into the pot. Cook for an additional 15 minutes over low heat, stirring frequently until the pudding is thick and glossy. Stir in the vanilla extract, if you didn't use a vanilla bean.

Chill the pudding: Transfer the pudding to a container and cool uncovered in the refrigerator for 15 minutes. Stir before serving.

INDIAN RICE PUDDING WITH SAFFRON, CASHEWS, AND SULTANAS (*KHEER*)

As there are many styles and family recipes for *kheer*, none can be called the definitive version. This one has the signature spices and aromas that seem to be in nearly every recipe, however: saffron, cardamom, and cinnamon.

MAKES 3 CUPS (720 ML) OR SIX SERVINGS. GLUTEN-FREE.

- 3 **cups (720 ml) whole milk, divided**

- **Generous pinch saffron threads (12 to 15 threads)**

- 1 **tablespoon (14 g) unsalted butter**

- ¼ **cup (30 g) cashew pieces, roughly chopped**

- ¼ **cup (40 g) golden raisins (sultanas)**

- ¼ **cup (46 g) basmati or long-grain rice**

- ½ **cup (120 ml) sweetened condensed milk**

- 4 **green cardamom pods, or ½ teaspoon cardamom powder**

- 1 **pod star anise**

- 1 **(3-inch / 7.5-cm) stick cinnamon**

- ¼ **teaspoon ground ginger**

- ½ **teaspoon salt**

- ¼ **cup (35 g) toasted pistachio nuts, shelled and finely chopped**

Steep the saffron: Warm ¼ cup (60 ml) of the milk in a small measuring cup and stir in the saffron. Set aside to steep.

Sauté the nuts and raisins: Melt the butter in a deep, lidded 3-quart (2.8-L) saucepan over medium-high heat. When the butter foams, add the cashew pieces, raisins, and rice. Sauté for 1 minute, or until the raisins and nuts are nicely toasted and golden.

Cook the rice: Stir in the remaining 2¾ cups milk and 1 cup (240 ml) water, the condensed milk, cardamom, star anise, cinnamon, and ginger, and bring to a boil on medium-high heat. Lower the heat and simmer, uncovered, for 20 minutes, stirring frequently. Cook until the rice is very tender and the milk has reduced slightly.

Sweeten the pudding: Stir in the salt and the saffron-steeped milk. Cook for an additional 5 minutes, then turn off the heat.

Chill the pudding: Transfer the pudding to a container and cool in the refrigerator for 15 minutes before serving. Garnish with a sprinkle of chopped pistachios.

INDIAN RICE PUDDING: WHAT MAKES A GREAT DISH OF KHEER?

Monica Bhide writes eloquently about her heritage of Indian cuisine. She is the author of **Modern Spice** and blogs at monicabhide.com. I turn to her books and blog frequently for advice on Indian cooking, and I wanted her thoughts about making the best possible dish of Indian *kheer*, an extra-rich, extra-smooth Indian rice pudding:

"Slow cooking is one of the secrets to a good kheer," Monica said. "Let the milk and the rice simmer together for a long time on low heat. I like mine thick, so I use sweetened condensed milk. This combination gives the kheer a lovely thick and creamy consistency. A perfect dish of kheer is always spiced just right: think saffron, think cardamom, think cinnamon—your call but make sure you use a seasoning to make the flavor really pop."

DARK CHOCOLATE AND ROSEWATER RICE PUDDING

Roses and chocolate are a romantic pairing of flavors, and one I learned from Alana Shock, a splendid chef in my hometown. Her chocolate-rosewater panna cotta inspired this recipe, with its dark chocolate richness and just a hint of rose fragrance. If you want to make it extra-special, splurge on a handful of candied rose petals to garnish the dish—these pretty edibles can be found through mail-order specialty food companies such as Market Hall Foods (see Sources, page 213). If rosewater isn't your thing, but you want the dark chocolate pudding, then substitute an extra teaspoon of vanilla. But I do urge you to try this as written; chocolate and roses are a wonderful combination.

MAKES 3 CUPS (720 ML) OR SIX SERVINGS. GLUTEN-FREE.

- ½ tablespoon (7 g) unsalted butter
- ½ cup (100 g) arborio or other short-grain rice
- 2 tablespoons cocoa powder
- 4 cups (960 ml) whole milk
- 3 tablespoons sugar
- 4 ounces (115 g) bittersweet chocolate, finely chopped
- 1 ounce (30 g) unsweetened chocolate, finely chopped
- 1¼ teaspoons rosewater (see Note, page 55)
- ½ teaspoon pure vanilla extract
- ¼ teaspoon kosher salt
- Unsweetened whipped cream, to serve

Toast the rice: Melt the butter in a heavy 3-quart (2.8-L) saucepan over medium-high heat. When it foams, add the rice and stir for 3 to 4 minutes, until it becomes golden and nearly translucent.

Cook the rice: Stir in the cocoa powder, then whisk in the milk. Bring to a boil, then lower the heat and cook, stirring frequently, for 25 minutes, or until the rice is quite tender and the milk has reduced to a soupy consistency.

Sweeten and thicken the pudding: Stir in the sugar and chocolates until they melt and are fully incorporated with the rice. Stir in the rosewater, vanilla, and salt and remove from the heat.

Chill the pudding: Transfer the pudding to a container and cool slightly in the refrigerator before serving.

Best served warm or at room temperature, with a dollop of unsweetened whipped cream.

FILIPINO CHAMPORADO: CHOCOLATE BREAKFAST PUDDING

"*Champorado* evokes many memories for every Filipino," says Elizabeth Besa Quirino, a Filipina food writer and blogger (find her at asianinamericamag.com). I was talking to her about the chocolate and coconut rice breakfast pudding that is, in some ways, the national dish of the Philippines. Like others, Elizabeth sees rice pudding as one of the most basic dishes of childhood comfort. "Nothing else fills the belly and warms the heart like a thick rice porridge with sweet coconut flavors, with robust chocolate and sugar." She says that this was a dish of memory and childhood, of parents making it on cold days in the winter and serving it for breakfast with salty dishes, like dried fish. Chocolate pudding for breakfast? Yes, please!

SALTED CARAMEL RISOTTO

I prefer caramel that flirts on the edge of burnt, especially in this rice pudding, which is inspired by classic Italian risotto. Here, cooked until it's very dark, with a smoky, bitter edge, the caramel balances the milky sweetness of the rice.

This is also an unusual pudding in that it forgoes much of the milkiness of the other grain puddings in this chapter. I cook the rice in water, with just a little milk. The liquid is gradually evaporated when the rice is mixed with the caramel, leaving an intensely flavored sauce. This is very rich pudding, but that quality comes almost entirely from the caramel itself—not the dairy.

MAKES 3 CUPS (720 ML) OR SIX SERVINGS. GLUTEN-FREE.

- ½ tablespoon (7 g) unsalted butter
- ½ cup (100 g) short-grain white rice, such as arborio
- 1 cup (240 ml) whole milk
- 1 cup (200 g) sugar
- 1 cup (240 ml) cream
- 1½ teaspoons pure vanilla extract
- ½ teaspoon kosher salt
- Unsweetened whipped cream, to serve

Toast the rice: Heat 2 cups (480 ml) water. Melt the butter in a heavy 3-quart (2.8-L) pan over medium-high heat. When the butter foams up, add the rice and cook for 3 to 4 minutes, stirring until it is translucent and golden.

Cook the rice: Pour in the milk and the hot water. Bring to a boil, then lower to a steady simmer and cook, stirring frequently, for 15 minutes, or until the rice grains have softened and are al dente (completely cooked through but still with some chewiness).

Make the caramel: While the rice is cooking, mix the sugar and ¼ cup (60 ml) water in a 4-quart (3.8-L) or larger heavy pot with tall sides. Cook over high heat, stirring, until the sugar dissolves and the mixture comes to a boil. Stop stirring and watch the syrup; when light golden streaks appear, carefully swirl the pot to help the sugar caramelize evenly. Continue boiling until the mixture turns a dark amber color. The sugar will begin to smoke; this is normal.

When the caramel has been smoking for about 15 seconds, pull the pan off the heat and carefully add the cream in a slow stream, whisking constantly. Be careful, as hot steam will bubble up furiously. Whisk this mixture until smoothly combined. (If the caramel seizes and becomes a solid mass when the cream is added, return the pan to low heat and continue whisking until it is melted and smooth. You can minimize the chance of seizing by heating the cream prior to pouring it in.)

Sweeten the rice: Add the rice to the caramel, stirring well. Simmer over medium-low heat, for 15 to 20 minutes, until much of the liquid has evaporated. Stir frequently to keep the rice from scorching.

The liquid will reduce and get darker, and the rice will soften a little more. The pudding will look soupy and thin, but it will thicken considerably as it cools. Stir in the vanilla and salt. Transfer to a container and refrigerate until the pudding is at your desired consistency and temperature—about 30 minutes for a warm pudding, and 2 hours for a cold pudding. (If the cold pudding is too firm, thin with a little whole milk.) Serve warm with unsweetened whipped cream.

GINGERED BROWN RICE PUDDING
WITH PLUM CONSERVE

Many people eat brown rice because of its nutritional benefits, but I prefer it to white rice simply because it tastes so much better. Those little pearls of rice have a pleasantly chewy texture when cooked, and their flavor is sweet and nutty. Here, that nuttiness is accentuated with fresh ginger's gentle heat. The plum conserve is juicy and sweet and plays deliciously with the spicy warmth of ginger in this pudding.

MAKES 3 CUPS (720 ML) OR
SIX SERVINGS. GLUTEN-FREE.

- 3½ cups (840-ml) reduced-fat (2%) or whole milk, divided
- ¾ cup (147 g) short-grain brown rice
- ½ teaspoon salt
- 1 2-inch (5-cm) piece fresh ginger, unpeeled and cut into thick coins
- ¼ cup (55 g) packed dark brown sugar
- 2 large egg yolks
- 1 teaspoon pure vanilla extract

Cook the rice: Combine ½ cup (120 ml) milk with 1 cup (240 ml) water in a lidded 3-quart (2.8-L) saucepan and bring to a boil over high heat. Stir in the rice and salt, and bring back to a boil. Cover and turn the heat to low. Cook for 40 minutes, or until the rice is tender and sticky.

Sweeten and thicken the pudding: Remove the lid and stir in the remaining 3 cups (720 ml) milk, along with the ginger and sugar, and bring to a simmer over medium-high heat. Cook, uncovered, stirring frequently, for 15 minutes, or until the pudding has a soupy consistency. In a separate small bowl, whisk the egg yolks. Stir in about 1 cup (240 ml) of the cooked pudding to temper the egg yolks, and slowly pour this back into the pan. Cook for an additional 3 to 5 minutes, until the pudding thickens a little more and looks glossy. Turn off the heat and stir in the vanilla.

Remove the ginger coins. Transfer the pudding to a serving dish or individual cups and serve warm or at room temperature with plum conserve (recipe follows).

PLUM CONSERVE

Plums are one of my favorite fruits, and I feel that they are often underrepresented in desserts. Here, their dark juiciness is complemented by golden raisins, ginger, and a little nip of rum.

MAKES 4 CUPS (960 ML).

- 1 pound (455 g) ripe red or black plums
- 1 cup (200 g) sugar
- 1 cup (160 g) golden raisins
- 1-inch (2.5-cm) piece fresh ginger, peeled and cut into thick coins
- Pinch salt
- 2 tablespoons rum (optional)

Stone the plums and roughly chop them into pieces about 1 inch (2.5 cm) to a side. Mix with the sugar, raisins, and ginger in a heavy saucepan. Bring to a boil over high heat, then lower the heat and simmer for 15 minutes, stirring frequently. When the sauce has reduced slightly, remove the pan from the heat and stir in the salt and rum, if using. Transfer to a lidded container and refrigerate for up to 1 month, or freeze for up to 1 year.

Serve at room temperature or heated to lukewarm in the microwave or on the stovetop.

THAI STICKY RICE
WITH MANGO AND SESAME SEEDS

The first time I ate Thai sticky rice with mango, I was in Los Angeles. A friend bought me a Styrofoam container of it from a street vendor. The rice was warm, and the glistening slices of mango glowed. I'll never forget the taste of sweet and salty sticky rice. I also will never forget the day I realized how easy it is to make this treat for myself.

MAKES SIX ½-CUP (720-ML) SERVINGS. GLUTEN-FREE. DAIRY-FREE.

- 2 **cups (370 g) Thai sticky or sweet rice, available in Asian groceries**
- 2 **(13.5-ounce / 400-ml) cans coconut milk, ideally a Thai brand such as Chaokoh**
- 6 **tablespoons (75 g) sugar, divided**
- 2 **teaspoons salt, divided**
- 1 **teaspoon cornstarch**
- 2 **ripe mangos**
- 3 **tablespoons toasted sesame seeds**

NOTE // This dessert depends on excellent mango. Look for small fruits, and let them get extremely ripe; they should smell sickly sweet and be soft. If such mangos cannot be had, this is also good with truly ripe peaches, slipped out of their fuzzy jackets with a quick dip in boiling water. The sweet fragrance of an August peach is North America's answer to mango.

Soak and steam the rice: Soak the rice in a bowl of water for 1 hour. Drain and rinse it thoroughly. Pour 2 cups (480 ml) water into a lidded 2-quart (2-L) saucepan and bring to a boil. Place the rice in a steamer insert inside the pan. Cover tightly and steam over low to medium heat for 20 minutes.

Make the rice sauce: While the rice is steaming, open the cans of coconut milk and spoon out the thick cream on top. Place in a small bowl. You should have approximately 1 cup (240 ml).

Pour the remaining thinner, lighter coconut milk into a small saucepan. (It will be a little over 1 cup / 240 ml.) Stir in ¼ cup (50 g) of the sugar and 1½ teaspoons of the salt. Warm over medium heat, stirring frequently, for 5 minutes. Do not let the sauce boil.

Sweeten the rice: Transfer the rice to a large bowl. The grains should be tender and shiny, and the rice will have formed thick clumps. Slowly, pour the warm coconut milk over the rice, stirring frequently. You want the milk to coat the rice but not leave puddles. Keep stirring, and stop adding coconut milk when it looks like the rice is saturated; you may not use it all. Set the rice aside for 15 minutes to finish absorbing the coconut milk.

Make the topping sauce: Rinse out the coconut milk saucepan and pour in the coconut cream. Stir in the remaining 2 tablespoons sugar and ½ teaspoon salt. In a separate bowl, whisk together 4 teaspoons water and the cornstarch. Whisk this slurry into the coconut cream and cook over low heat for about 3 minutes, or until the mixture thickens considerably. Set aside.

Cut the mangos: First cut off the bottom of each mango so it can stand upright. Slice away the skin in thin strips, until the mango is completely peeled. Cut off the flesh in slices, starting with the broad cheeks on each side, then the thinner strips that remain.

To serve, place ½ cup (120 ml) rice on each of six plates and arrange mango slices around it. Drizzle with the coconut topping and sprinkle ½ tablespoon toasted sesame seeds on top. Serve warm.

WHAT *IS* TAPIOCA ANYWAY?

Frogspawn. Tadpole eyes. Goo! Tapioca's texture lends itself to some pretty unappealing nicknames, but those of us who love these jellied pearls, swimming in sweet milk pudding, know that these only add to its old-fashioned charm.

Tapioca is made from the root of the cassava plant, also known as yuca and manioc. Cassava is a staple around the world, but especially in warm regions; it is grown widely in South America, Thailand, and parts of Africa, particularly Nigeria. To make the pearls we know as tapioca, starch is extracted from the root of the plant and powdered, then formed into balls. Tapioca has incredible thickening power, and it swells quickly in water.

Tapioca pudding, when done right, has a smooth, custardy base with delicate pearls of fully cooked tapioca suspended in the custard. It shouldn't be gummy or too thick.

OLD-FASHIONED TAPIOCA PUDDING

Here's a very simple recipe for tapioca pudding. It uses the regular, not quick-cooking, tapioca pearls (I like the Bob's Red Mill brand), with a shortcut to help the process go much faster than you would expect: I precook my tapioca in water, instead of soaking it overnight as is traditional. This is definitely an unorthodox method, but I love it. It gives you real, pearly tapioca pudding in just thirty minutes. It also leaves the pearls discrete, with a good chew, which I prefer.

MAKES 4 CUPS (960 ML)
OR EIGHT SERVINGS.
GLUTEN-FREE.

- ⅔ cup (117 g) small tapioca pearls
- 2 cups (480 ml) whole milk
- 3 large egg yolks
- ½ cup (100 g) sugar
- ½ cup (120 ml) cream
- 1 teaspoon salt
- 1½ teaspoons pure vanilla extract

Precook the tapioca: Put the tapioca in a lidded 2-quart (2-L) saucepan and add enough water just to cover. Bring to a boil over medium heat. Turn the heat off and cover for 15 minutes. When you remove the lid, you'll see that the tapioca will have swollen up into what appears to be one solid mass.

Cook the tapioca: Pour in the milk gradually, using a large whisk to break up the chunks of tapioca. Bring to a simmer, then turn the heat down to low. Cook, whisking very frequently to loosen the tapioca and keep the bottom from scorching. When the milk has reduced slightly and the pudding looks thicker, about 5 minutes, turn off the heat.

Make an egg yolk slurry: In a separate small bowl, whisk together the egg yolks, sugar, and cream.

Temper the slurry: Add about 1 cup (240 ml) of the hot tapioca mixture and whisk until combined. Slowly pour the tempered slurry back into the pot, counting to 10 as you pour. Whisk to combine.

Thicken the pudding: Bring the mixture back to a simmer over medium heat, stirring constantly. Cook for 5 minutes more over low heat, stirring frequently. The pearls will become translucent, and the pudding will thicken.

Flavor the pudding: Remove the pan from the heat and whisk in the salt and vanilla. Serve the pudding warm or chilled. To refrigerate it, spread it in a container and place plastic wrap or buttered wax paper directly on the surface to cover it.

QUICKER TAPIOCA PUDDING

Making tapioca pudding can be a time-consuming process. If you want your pudding faster, without having to precook the pearls, then use this recipe, which calls for quick tapioca. Quick, or "minute," tapioca is tapioca flour that has been precooked and formed into small pearls. These are usually smaller than regular tapioca pearls, and they cook much faster, but sometimes they are a little gummier.

MAKES 3 CUPS (720 ML) OR SIX SERVINGS. GLUTEN-FREE.

- 3 cups (720 ml) whole milk
- ½ cup (100 g) sugar
- ¼ cup (48 g) quick or minute tapioca
- 1 large egg yolk
- 1 teaspoon pure vanilla extract
- ¼ teaspoon salt

Cook the tapioca: Whisk together the milk, sugar, tapioca, and egg yolk in a 2-quart (2-L) or larger saucepan. Let stand for 5 minutes. Bring to a boil over low heat, stirring frequently. When the mixture comes to a full rolling boil, turn off the heat. Whisk in the vanilla extract and salt. Let the pudding rest for at least 20 minutes in the pan. It will still be relatively thin, but it will continue to thicken as it chills in the fridge. To refrigerate, spread the pudding in a container and place plastic wrap or buttered wax paper directly on the surface to cover it. Best eaten within 3 days.

VIETNAMESE COCONUT TAPIOCA PUDDING
WITH BANANA (CHÈ CHUỐI)

I lived in Orlando, Florida, for a few years, and while I was there, I discovered that the city had a lot more to offer than just Mickey Mouse (who doesn't really live there, anyway). There's a robust Vietnamese community downtown, and on my weekly trips to a *bánh mì* shop nearby, I would always get a plastic cup of tapioca pudding to follow my sandwich. The tapioca was cooked in coconut milk and mixed with chunks of banana. It was like upscale children's food, simple and wholesome and not too sweet. This recipe reproduces it note for note; it's my own comfort pudding.

MAKES 3 CUPS (720 ML) OR SIX SERVINGS. GLUTEN-FREE. DAIRY-FREE.

- 1 (13.5-ounce / 400-ml) can coconut milk
- ½ cup (88 g) small tapioca pearls
- 3 to 4 small ripe bananas, peeled, halved lengthwise, and cut into 1-inch (2.5-cm) pieces
- ½ teaspoon salt
- 2 tablespoons granulated sugar
- 2 tablespoons packed dark brown sugar

  Unsweetened coconut flakes, to garnish

Cook the tapioca: Bring 3 cups (720 ml) water and the coconut milk to a boil in a 2-quart (2-L) or larger saucepan. Stir in the tapioca pearls and lower the heat to a simmer. Cook for 13 to 15 minutes, until the tapioca pearls are translucent and tender. Stir frequently to make sure the tapioca doesn't stick to the bottom of the pan.

Sweeten and flavor the pudding: Add the bananas, salt, and both sugars, and cook for an additional 3 to 4 minutes, until the bananas are warmed through. Refrigerate in a covered container. The pudding can be served lukewarm in 30 minutes, or chill it for 2 hours and eat it cold. Serve it with coconut flakes sprinkled on top.

CREAMY LEMON-COCONUT QUINOA PUDDING

It is perhaps not strictly correct to begin this section of whole-grain puddings with a quinoa pudding, as quinoa is technically not a grain at all, but the edible seed of a leafy plant related to spinach and beets. But it is used like a grain, and because it is a significant source of complete protein, gluten-free, and high in fiber, it has become incredibly popular.

These dietary wonders aside, I enjoy quinoa's delicate texture; its tiny orbs fluff up when cooked, but preserve a nuttiness and a little pop in the mouth. In this pudding, they actually taste quite a bit like tapioca, but with a little more chew.

MAKES 3 CUPS (720 ML) OR SIX SERVINGS. GLUTEN-FREE.

- ¾ cup (128 g) regular (golden) quinoa
- 2 cups (480 ml) whole milk
- 1 cup (240 ml) cream
- ⅓ cup (75 g) packed brown sugar
- 2 lemons, zested and juiced (about 6 tablespoons / 90 ml juice)
- ½ teaspoon ground ginger
- 2 large egg yolks
- 1 teaspoon pure vanilla extract
- ½ teaspoon salt
- ¾ cup (67 g) shredded sweetened coconut, lightly toasted

Rinse the quinoa: Soak the quinoa in a bowl of cold water for at least 15 minutes, then rinse it for 3 to 4 minutes under running water and drain. (This removes the bitterness of the natural protective coating. This is generally removed from commercially available quinoa, but I find that it is still good to soak and rinse it, because some bitterness does linger, and it helps the dish to cook up fluffier.)

Cook the quinoa: Stir the quinoa together with the milk, cream, sugar, and lemon zest in a 2-quart (2-L) saucepan. Add the ginger. Bring to a boil over medium-high heat, then lower to a simmer and cook, stirring frequently, for 20 minutes, or until the quinoa is tender. You will notice that the germ will spring out from the seed, like a tiny curl. This is a good way to tell by sight if the quinoa is fully cooked.

Thicken and flavor the pudding: Whisk the egg yolks thoroughly in a small bowl and stir in about 1 cup (240 ml) of the cooked quinoa. Slowly pour the tempered egg yolks back into the pot, stirring constantly. Cook for an additional 3 to 5 minutes, until the pudding is a little thicker and has turned glossy. Stir in the vanilla, salt, lemon juice, and ½ cup (45 g) of the coconut, and refrigerate in a separate container. Serve warm or cold, garnished with the remaining toasted coconut.

EASY FLAVOR VARIATION
dairy-free lemon-coconut quinoa pudding

You can also make this dairy-free (and vegan) by substituting two 13.5-ounce (400-ml) cans of full-fat coconut milk for the milk and cream. Omit the egg yolks. Otherwise, make the recipe as directed above.

My friend Maria Speck wrote a book called *Ancient Grains for Modern Meals*, which celebrates the deliciousness of whole grains. It has been extremely popular and when I was developing these recipes, I couldn't think of anyone more knowledgeable or passionate about whole grains.

I asked Maria about her favorite grains for pudding, and why. "Two whole grains lend themselves beautifully to comforting puddings," she told me. "One is Chinese black rice, a soft-textured rice once only served to the emperors of China. Not only does it turn a gorgeous deep burgundy color when cooked, the grain also remains supple when chilled. For the same reason, I also love making millet pudding, which has a similar texture to rice pudding. I make sure not to tell anyone about the 'secret ingredient,' as I don't want to be accused of serving bird food. Once everyone licks their bowl clean, the pleasure is all mine."

She also offered advice for creating an impromptu pudding out of a favorite cooked grain: "Many grains harden when chilled, so leftovers should always be warmed on the stovetop or in the microwave. If I cook grain for breakfast, I often infuse it with spices such as a whole cinnamon stick or aniseeds. This will give you a head start when transforming the leftovers into sweet puddings, as your grain already has a wonderful subtle aroma."

PISTACHIO AND VERMICELLI PUDDING
(PAYASAM)

This thin Indian pudding substitutes very delicate noodles for rice or whole grains, and it has a delicious, unusual texture. It's one of my favorite puddings. You can find *semiya*, the short, thin noodles used in this pudding, at Indian groceries and online (see Sources, page 213). If these are not available, use the thinnest angel hair pasta you can find.

MAKES 3 CUPS (720 ML) OR SIX SERVINGS.

- 2 tablespoons (28 g) ghee or unsalted butter, divided
- 1 cup *semiya* or angel hair noodles broken into 2-inch (5-cm) lengths
- 2 cups (480 ml) reduced-fat (2%) or whole milk
- ½ teaspoon salt
- 1 (14-ounce / 397-g) can sweetened condensed milk
- ½ teaspoon cardamom powder
- ½ cup (62 g) pistachio nutmeats
- ¼ cup (40 g) golden raisins (sultanas)

Toast the noodles: Heat a large skillet over high heat and add 1 tablespoon of the ghee. When the pan is hot, add the noodles and cook, stirring, for 2 to 3 minutes, until they are golden and toasted.

Cook the pudding: Stir the milk, 2 cups (480 ml) water, and the salt together in a 2-quart (2-L) or larger saucepan and bring to a boil. Stir in the toasted noodles and lower to a simmer. Cook for 6 minutes, or until the noodles are just cooked through. Stir in the condensed milk and cardamom and simmer for an additional 15 minutes, or until the pudding is creamy.

Toast the nuts and raisins: Meanwhile, heat the remaining ghee in the skillet over high heat. Add the pistachios and raisins and cook for 1 minute, or just until golden and fragrant. Stir the pistachios and raisins into the pudding. Pour into a separate container and chill.

Serve lukewarm or at room temperature. If you have refrigerated leftovers, you may need to thin the chilled pudding with a little extra milk before serving.

COFFEE, ALMOND, AND DATE MILLET PUDDING

Millet is perhaps best known in North America as a common ingredient in birdseed mix! This is a pity because it is delicious and nutritious for humans as well as feathered folk. It contains about the same amount of protein as wheat, but it is gluten-free and high in fiber and nutrients. This pudding plays up millet's delicate pearl grains with earthy, coffee-flavored almond milk and the sweetness of dates. This is not a very rich pudding—it would be perfectly respectable at the breakfast table.

MAKES 3 CUPS (720 ML) OR SIX SERVINGS. GLUTEN-FREE. DAIRY-FREE.

- 3 **cups (720 ml) vanilla almond milk**
- ¼ **cup (21 g) roasted coffee beans, roughly chopped or ground**
- ¾ **cup (141 g) millet**
- 1 **teaspoon olive oil**
- ¼ **teaspoon salt**
- ¼ **cup (55 g) packed brown sugar**
- ¾ **cup (114 g) whole pitted dates, roughly chopped**
- 1 **tablespoon (14 g) unsalted butter (optional—omit for a dairy-free pudding)**
- **Nutmeg, to serve**

Steep the coffee in the almond milk: In a saucepan over medium heat, warm the almond milk to just under boiling. Turn off the heat and stir in the coffee beans. Set aside to steep for 4 minutes, then strain out the coffee beans. Discard the beans, and set the milk aside.

Toast the millet: Rinse the millet for 4 to 5 minutes in a fine-mesh sieve and drain well. Heat the oil in a lidded 3-quart (2.8-L) saucepan over medium-high heat and add the millet. Cook for 5 minutes, stirring and shaking the pan, until the millet is toasted.

Cook the millet: Add 2 cups (480 ml) water and the salt. Bring to a boil, then lower the heat and cover the pan. Simmer for 20 minutes, until millet is tender.

Sweeten and flavor the pudding: Add the sugar, the almond milk, and the dates to the millet and stir to combine.

Thicken the pudding: Return to a simmer and cook for about 15 minutes more, until the liquid has reduced slightly and the pudding looks creamy. If desired, stir in the butter to make the pudding slightly richer. Transfer to a container and serve warm or chilled, with a dusting of nutmeg.

WALNUT, FIG, AND BARLEY PUDDING

Barley is one of my favorite grains. Its tender chewiness adds a delicious bite to so many traditional soups and stews. But barley isn't just for dinner; it makes a wonderful pudding, too. Here, barley's nutty flavor is highlighted with figs, walnuts, and orange zest for a warm pudding that is just right for autumn.

- 1 tablespoon (14 g) unsalted butter
- ½ cup (60 g) finely chopped walnuts
- ⅓ cup (60 g) pearled barley
- 3 cups (720 ml) whole milk
- ½ teaspoon salt
- ⅛ teaspoon cinnamon
- ¼ cup (60 ml) cream
- 3 tablespoons dark brown sugar
- 3 large egg yolks
- Grated zest of 1 small orange
- 1 tablespoon brandy (optional)
- ⅔ cup (100 g) dried figs, roughly chopped
- Whipped cream (see page 167), to serve

Toast the nuts and barley: Heat the butter in a 3-quart (2.8-L) saucepan over medium-high heat and add the walnuts. Cook for 2 to 3 minutes, until they are well toasted. Remove the walnuts and set aside. Add the barley to the pan and continue cooking over medium-high heat unti it is toasted and fragrant, about 2 minutes.

Parboil the barley: Add 2 cups (480 ml) water and bring to a boil. Boil uncovered for 15 minutes, stirring occasionally.

Cook the barley: Pour the milk into the pan with the barley and water. Add the salt and cinnamon and stir. Bring to a boil and lower to a simmer. Cook, uncovered, over low heat for 45 minutes, or until the barley is soft but still al dente and the milk has reduced slightly. Stir occasionally to make sure the barley doesn't stick to the pan.

Thicken and sweeten the pudding: In a separate small bowl, whisk together the cream, sugar, and egg yolks. Add 1 cup (240 ml) of the hot barley to this bowl and whisk. Slowly add this mixture back into the pan, whisking vigorously. Continue cooking for 1 to 2 minutes, whisking frequently, until the pudding has thickened slightly. Stir in the orange zest and brandy, if using, as well as the reserved walnuts and chopped figs.

Transfer to a serving dish, let cool for 15 minutes, and serve warm with a dollop of whipped cream.

CRANACHAN (SCOTTISH OAT PUDDING)

One way to use oats in a puddinglike dessert is the classic Scottish dish *cranachan*. To make it, toast about ½ cup (48 g) regular rolled oats in 1 tablespoon unsalted butter melted in a wide skillet. Cook until the oats are toasted and very fragrant. Whip 2 cups (480 ml) cream with 2 tablespoons warmed honey until it holds soft peaks. Fold in 3 tablespoons Scotch or Drambuie. Fold the toasted oats into the whipped cream, reserving a few tablespoons for garnish. Layer the oats in a parfait dish, alternating them with fresh strawberries or raspberries.

PANNA COTTA & OTHER GELLED PUDDINGS

This chapter offers recipes for panna cotta and other gelled puddings—each of them different from the cornstarch puddings in the first chapter in that they are lighter, colder, and a little simpler to make. The first among these, panna cotta, is a simple yet sophisticated Italian pudding made with cream, sugar, and gelatin. Gelatin desserts like panna cotta have a very smooth texture, and they are ready quickly, because most of the liquid in them does not need to be heated. Melted gelatin is stirred in, and they are set to chill in the fridge.

Straight-up panna cotta isn't the only pudding you can make with gelatin. Some of my favorite puddings fall into a cloudy, delicious area between panna cotta, whipped cream, and gelatin. From a Champagne-marshmallow cloud studded with pistachios to jellied yogurt squares with hot-pink raspberry syrup, this chapter also includes some of these easy and unusual desserts.

ALL ABOUT GELATIN

Gelatin is a key ingredient in many of the puddings in this book. It's also the magic ingredient that gives Jell-O and other jellies their firmness. Gelatin is a highly processed yet natural substance made from the collagen in the bones and skin of animals and fish.

THE ESSENTIALS OF USING GELATIN

Gelatin isn't difficult to work with, but here are a few essentials you should know:

- » Gelatin, when dissolved in liquid and chilled, turns solid. The consistency depends on the quantity of gelatin used and how long it has been chilled.

- » The longer you chill gelatin, the firmer it gets! This is why many gelatin-based desserts taste soft and delicate on the first day they're made, but rubbery on the fourth.

- » Gelatin melts at about human body temperature, which is why fruit jellies and panna cotta have that pleasing melt-in-your-mouth texture.

- » Before dissolving, gelatin needs to be softened, or bloomed, in water. This helps saturate the gelatin crystals with moisture and prepares the gelatin for dissolving completely.

WORKING WITH GELATIN

Forms of Gelatin: Powder, Sheets, Leaves?

Gelatin is sold in different forms in different parts of the world. In the United States, it is most commonly sold in powdered form, in ¼-ounce (7-g) packets that contain about 2¼ teaspoons apiece. Professional pastry chefs usually prefer sheet or leaf gelatin in the form of small, translucent sheets; these are more commonly found in Europe. Pastry chefs and cooks I talked with feel that these sheets are easier to work with than powdered gelatin, which takes longer to dissolve.

I wanted to stick with what is commonly available in the United States, however, so these recipes are formulated for powdered gelatin. It is not only the form most cooks here are familiar with, but it is also more standardized than sheet gelatin, which comes in a range of strengths.

Measuring Gelatin

Many recipes measure gelatin simply in packets or envelopes, as in "1 envelope powdered gelatin." But standard-size gelatin packets can vary widely in volume, even if they have the same weight. I've measured packets that contain anywhere from 1¾ teaspoons all the way up to nearly 1 tablespoon. So my recipes call for specific *teaspoon* volumes of gelatin.

If you're left with an opened packet of gelatin after making one of these recipes, seal it in a plastic bag and put it back in the cupboard to use later. It won't spoil.

Basic Proportions of Gelatin to Liquid

When deciding how much gelatin to use, it's always a game of chicken between cook and gelatin! You obviously want to use enough to make your ingredients gel into a substantial, solid dessert. But you don't want to use too much—too much gelatin, and you get a rubbery hockey puck.

Here are the basic proportions I use for desserts. These will vary slightly between recipes, depending on the amount of acid and fat present in the mixture to be set.

- » For a very soft mixture with fat in it, like creamy panna cotta:
  about ⅔ teaspoon powdered gelatin per cup (240 ml) of liquid.

- » For a firmer mixture with fat in it, like molded panna cotta:
  about 1¼ teaspoons powdered gelatin per cup (240 ml) of liquid.

- » For a soft, nonfatty liquid, like fruit jelly served in cups:
  1 teaspoon powdered gelatin per cup (240 ml) of liquid.

- » For a very firm nonfatty liquid, like molded fruit jelly:
  2 teaspoons powdered gelatin per cup (240 ml) of liquid.

Tips for Setting Gelatin Faster

If you're in a rush, here are a few tips for hurrying gelatin along:

- » Chill or freeze the mold or cups before pouring the mixture in.

- » Stir the gelatin mixture in a bowl set in an ice bath until it gets slushy and cold.

Do not freeze gelatin, as this destroys its thickening power. From time to time, a recipe may instruct you to quick-chill a gelatin in the freezer, but never for more than 15 minutes.

Fruit Enzymes and Acids in Jellies

Certain fruits contain a family of enzymes that inhibit gelatin's thickening and setting properties. These include pineapple, kiwifruit, papaya, and figs. Several of these, most notably pineapple and kiwifruit, are used as meat tenderizers, and breaking down meat-derived proteins is obviously not a good thing when trying to set gelatin (which is basically a meat protein—see how this is a problem?). So if you are using fruit or juice from any of these, you will need to heat it first to deactivate the enzyme.

This enzyme does not, however, present a problem when working with agar or other vegetable-based thickeners.

Other fruit, like lemons and limes, contain a lot of acid, and this can interfere with gelatin setting properly. Where necessary, I've adjusted gelatin proportions to allow for this.

BASIC METHOD FOR GELATIN-BASED DESSERTS

Here are the basic steps for working with gelatin in making panna cotta, gelled puddings, and fruit jellies:

1 **Soften the gelatin:** Gelatin always needs to be softened (or *bloomed*) in cold liquid before dissolving. Most of these recipes instruct you to use milk for this, which will take a little longer than water. To soften the gelatin, shake it evenly over the surface of the liquid, and let it sit for 5 to 10 minutes, or until the surface has gone soft and wrinkled. The gelatin powder should darken and look saturated with the liquid.

2 **Warm and dissolve the gelatin:** Warm the gelatin gently over low or medium heat. The more slowly you dissolve it, the better it will set up. Stir frequently during this time. It will turn into a mushy liquid like applesauce, then quickly turn translucent and dissolve. It's very important that the gelatin dissolve completely. Use a spoon to wash the milk, water, or juice up against the side of the pan, and observe as it runs down—do you still see tiny granules? If so, keep warming. Lift and pour spoonfuls back into the pan, watching to see if it is fully dissolved. Do not boil, however—this destroys gelatin's thickening power. Honestly, this dissolving process doesn't take long (3 to 4 minutes at most), and it's not tricky at all. It took me longer to write this paragraph than it would have to dissolve a few teaspoons of gelatin!

3 **Dissolve the sugar with the gelatin:** Whisk the sugar, if called for, into the gelatin mixture and keep stirring over low heat until it is completely dissolved.

4 **Combine the sugar and gelatin solution with the rest of the liquid:** At this point, you can whisk the gelatin solution together with the cream or the rest of the liquid. Make sure the remaining liquid is at room temperature; you don't want to whisk warm gelatin directly into very cold liquid, as that can cause it to seize up and form "ropes" in the final product.

5 **Pour the mixture into a shallow container or cups and chill:** At this point the gelatin mixture can be chilled. The more shallow the pan or dish, the faster the gelatin will set up.

VEGETARIAN, VEGAN, AND KOSHER ISSUES

Gelatin is made from the collagen found in animal bones and skin, which are processed extensively to extract the essential proteins. Gelatin works on the same principles that make homemade chicken stock turn to jelly when refrigerated (a sign of good stock!). The silky, luxurious, melt-in-your-mouth texture of real gelatin comes only from animal products, unfortunately; scientists haven't been able to devise an equally good vegetarian substitute.

If you keep kosher or avoid pork products, you can buy all-beef gelatin or kosher gelatin, which is usually made from fish.

If you are a strict vegetarian or vegan and avoid all gelatin, then your options are limited. There are many vegetarian gelatin substitutes on the market, but they don't really have the same texture as regular gelatin.

VEGETARIAN AND VEGAN GELATIN SUBSTITUTES

If you do want to try a vegetarian alternative to gelatin, here are the best two products and the methods for their use. There are other vegan gels, but these are the two that I like best.

Unflavored Vegan Jel by Natural Desserts

What is it? A blend of vegetable gums and tapioca starch.

Substitute for 1 teaspoon gelatin: A generous 1½ teaspoons Vegan Jel.

Mouthfeel and taste: This is where Vegan Jel excels. Jelly made with it melts in your mouth, soft-set and wobbly. In fact, I think I prefer the texture of Vegan Jel to regular gelatin. It sets a bit softer though, so while it would be fine to use it for unmolded desserts, it would take a little bit of tweaking for a molded dessert like panna cotta. There's no measurable taste; it's flavorless.

Pros and cons: I think that Vegan Jel is by far the best vegan substitute for gelatin, given how easy it is to work with and the fact that it has a very similar mouthfeel. Its only drawback: cost. A box contains only one ⅓-ounce (10-g) envelope, which sets 2 cups (480 ml) of liquid, and each box costs between two and three dollars. So creating a larger dessert with Vegan Jel would be more costly than one made with regular gelatin.

Agar Agar

What is it? Agar agar is a seaweed product, and it is used in many Asian desserts and gels.

Substitute for 1 teaspoon gelatin: 1 teaspoon powdered agar agar.

Mouthfeel and taste: Agar agar sets firmer than gelatin, and it doesn't melt in your mouth the way gelatin does. Because it melts at a much higher temperature, it stays hard and chewy, breaking down into smaller and smaller crumbles as you chew. Its taste is neutral, like gelatin.

Pros and cons: The most notable (and widely used) vegetarian gelatin substitute, agar agar is derived from seaweed. It is easy to use, and it sets up at room temperature, so you don't even have to refrigerate it. The downside is its chewy, almost crunchy mouthfeel. It is also much trickier to unmold these desserts. You can find agar agar in health food stores and Asian groceries.

ALL ABOUT PANNA COTTA

WHAT IS PANNA COTTA?

In Italian, *panna cotta* means simply "cooked cream." And that's all it really is: cream warmed and thickened with gelatin, sweetened with a little sugar. Sure, you can make it fancier (and sweeter) than this, but that's the heart of it. The dessert originated in northern Italy, but it has spread widely. You'll find softly set cream puddings in restaurants all over the world.

These puddings can be light, with yogurt or milk balancing the cream—or extremely luxurious, draped in caramel and chocolate. Their defining characteristic is a pure, smooth texture.

WHY PANNA COTTA MAY BE THE PERFECT DESSERT

I have always wondered why people don't make panna cotta more frequently. It's so *easy*. A friend who is a very accomplished cook was visiting for dinner one evening, and I described how to make panna cotta. "You just warm up some milk and cream with sugar, and dissolve some gelatin, and put it in the fridge. It takes five minutes." My friend was flabbergasted. "I had no idea," she said. "I always assumed it was difficult!"

Panna cotta is definitely not difficult, and it is versatile, timewise. You can make it ahead of time, as an easy dessert you pull out of the fridge with no fuss, no muss. But if you're short on time, it's a great last-minute dessert, too. You can pour it into shallow dishes, and it will be set up before you're finished eating dinner.

Since it's made with only gelatin, sugar, milk, cream, and flavorings, panna cotta is naturally gluten-free. It is also much more adaptable to nondairy milks, like coconut and almond, so it's good for dairy-free folks. It can be made with fruit juice instead of milk, too, mixed with cream for a lighter, fresher pudding with no added sugar. It can be made low-fat or even no-fat.

It's truly just about the perfect dessert!

MILK, CREAM, AND FAT IN PANNA COTTA

I feel that the best panna cotta has an equal amount of cream and milk (I call for 2 percent milk, but any milk fat will do here). Some may disagree; they may feel that it's too rich. That's fine—feel free to experiment with the ratio of milk and cream that you prefer. The gelatin quantity will stay more or less the same, unless you remove the cream entirely. In that case, add an additional 1/2 teaspoon gelatin for a total of 2¾ teaspoons in the basic panna cotta recipe.

WHAT MAKES A PERFECT ITALIAN PANNA COTTA?

Domenica Marchetti is the author of many irresistible books about Italian food and cooking (how do you pass up something called **The Glorious Pasta of Italy**?). I asked for her thoughts on panna cotta—what makes her swoon when it comes to this very Italian pudding?

"Panna cotta, to me," Domenica said, "is the purest of the Italian spoon desserts [**dolci al cucchiaio**], comprising just four ingredients: cream, sugar, vanilla, and gelatin. The quality of the cream makes a difference, so when I make it, I always splurge and buy good, fresh, local cream that is pasteurized rather than ultra-pasteurized, and I use vanilla bean rather than extract. The hardest part about making panna cotta is achieving the proper consistency and texture—it should be silky smooth and just firm, with a gentle wobble."

"While I'm fond of variations such as lemon or espresso, I prefer the classic vanilla, served with a fresh seasonal fruit sauce (rhubarb is my favorite; it's pretty and its tart flavor is a nice contrast to the rich cream)."

HOW TO MAKE ANY PANNA COTTA DAIRY-FREE

Panna cotta is much more amenable to alternative dairies than cooked puddings and custards. Fat is less of an issue here, since the gelatin does most of the work of thickening the pudding.

If you want to replace some of the dairy with almond milk or rice milk, but aren't averse to having some cream in your pudding, simply replace the milk in any of these recipes with the milk of your choice. (You can also substitute fruit juice.) The gelatin amount will remain the same.

If, however, you want to substitute alternative dairy entirely, I recommend almond or rice milk, since they heat better than soy milk. Also, know that the pudding will be somewhat thinner and looser with no cream. Increase the total amount of gelatin to $2\frac{3}{4}$ teaspoons to compensate.

HOW TO UNMOLD PANNA COTTA

If you plan to unmold panna cotta on a plate (a very elegant presentation, yet so easy!) then follow these steps:

» Use small cups—panna cotta is easier to turn out of a small mold.

» Grease the ramekins or dessert cups very lightly with flavorless vegetable oil, then wipe most of the oil out with a clean paper towel.

» Make the panna cotta as directed in the basic panna cotta recipe, but use a total of $3\frac{1}{2}$ teaspoons gelatin.

» Let the panna cotta set for at least 6 hours, but ideally overnight.

» Before unmolding, let the panna cotta stand at room temperature for 15 minutes. Run a thin flexible knife around the inside of the cup to release the top edge, then quickly invert it onto a plate.

» If the panna cotta doesn't come out immediately, run the bottom of the dessert cup under warm water for a few moments, then try again.

PANNA COTTA TROUBLESHOOTING

» **Oh no! There are lumps in my panna cotta!** If there are lumps in your panna cotta, it means that your gelatin didn't dissolve completely. Make sure to completely liquefy it over low heat.

» **My panna cotta never got thick!** See above. Did you fully dissolve the gelatin? If so, has the panna cotta chilled for at least two to four hours? Also, remember that gelatin should never be boiled; this destroys its setting properties.

PANNA COTTA PARFAITS

Panna cotta makes beautiful layered desserts, especially when combined with fruit jellies like those in chapter 5. Here are some tips to successfully create lovely layered desserts:

1 Freeze the glass or container so it is really chilled before you begin to layer.

2 Start with a layer of jelly or fresh fruit or a chilled sauce, like caramel or fudge. Chill the bottom layer while you finish making the panna cotta, and let the panna cotta mixture cool a bit.

3 Pour the lukewarm panna cotta mixture over the layer, using a back-and-forth or circular motion, so it doesn't spill through the first layer.

4 Chill each layer of panna cotta or jelly for at least 20 minutes before adding the next layer.

Here are some ideas for combining fruit jelly flavors and panna cotta.

» **Classic Italian Soda** = Raspberry Jelly + Vanilla Panna Cotta

» **Caffè Macchiato** = Coffee Jelly + Almond-Amaretto Panna Cotta

» **Apple Pie** = Apple Cider Jelly + Sour Cream Panna Cotta

» **Chocolate Dreamsicle** = Orange Juice Jelly + Milky Chocolate Panna Cotta

» **The Tropics** = Mango Blender Mousse + Pineapple, Vanilla, and Coconut Panna Cotta

» **Sweet Tart** = Passion Fruit Jelly + Vanilla Panna Cotta

» **Perfect Summer** = Strawberry-Rhubarb Fruit Puree + Peach and Buttermilk Panna Cotta + Fresh Strawberries

» **Carrot Cake** = Carrot and Orange Juice Jelly + Strawberry Yogurt Panna Cotta + Toasted Walnuts

» **Clafoutis** = Cherry Juice Jelly + Vanilla Panna Cotta + Graham Cracker Crumbles

» **Piña Colada** = Pineapple Juice Jelly + Pineapple, Vanilla, and Coconut Panna Cotta + Toasted Coconut

VANILLA PANNA COTTA

Perfect panna cotta is not rubbery or thick. It should *wobble* when nudged with a spoon. This basic recipe gives what I consider the ideal proportions for a soft, delicate, creamy panna cotta in a cup. If you want to unmold the pudding on a plate, you'll need a touch more gelatin—see the instructions on page 102.

MAKES SIX ½-CUP (120-ML) SERVINGS. GLUTEN-FREE.

- 1½ **cups (360 ml) reduced-fat (2%) milk**
- 2¼ **teaspoons powdered gelatin**
- ⅓ **cup (65 g) sugar**
- 1½ **cups (360 ml) cream**
    Pinch salt
- 1 **vanilla bean, or 1 teaspoon pure vanilla extract**

Pour the milk into a 2-quart (2-L) saucepan and sprinkle the gelatin over the top. Set aside for 5 minutes to allow the gelatin to soften. Warm over medium heat, stirring constantly, until the gelatin is fully dissolved. Check the back of the spoon or tilt the pan up so that liquid runs up the side, and look for distinct granules. If you see them, the gelatin is not yet fully dissolved.

Stir the sugar into the milk and continue warming until it dissolves as well. Meanwhile, if you're using the vanilla bean, open it and scrape the seeds into the milk (see Note on page 33). Whisk the mixture so the seeds are incorporated into the liquid. (It should look speckled, like milk after an Oreo has been dunked in it repeatedly!)

Turn off the heat. Whisk in the cream, salt, and vanilla extract, if you're using that instead of a vanilla bean.

Divide this mixture among six ramekins or dessert glasses. Cover the glasses lightly with plastic wrap. Refrigerate the panna cotta and let it set for at least 2 hours—but preferably overnight, especially if you plan to unmold it. (If so, see the instructions on page 102.) The panna cotta can be made up to 3 days ahead and stored, covered in the refrigerator.

basic panna cotta adaptations

Instead of using the milk, substitute an equal amount of

- » low-fat yogurt
- » buttermilk
- » fruit juice or puree

earl grey panna cotta parfait

Make panna cotta as directed above, but steep 4 Earl Grey tea bags in the warmed milk with the gelatin and sugar for 5 minutes before proceeding to add the cream.

Parfait Suggestion: Serve layered with Scarlet Rose and Berry Pudding (page 55).

meyer lemon panna cotta parfait

Make panna cotta as directed above, but stir the zest of 2 Meyer lemons into the warmed milk before proceeding to add the cream.

Parfait Suggestion: Serve topped with Meyer Lemon Curd (page 172) and blueberries.

honey-lavender panna cotta

Make panna cotta as directed above, but substitute ¼ cup (60 ml) honey for the sugar and stir 2 teaspoons dried food-grade lavender buds into the milk. Warm until bubbles form around the edge, then turn off the heat and steep for 5 minutes. Strain out the lavender and proceed with the recipe. Serve with sliced strawberries or raspberries.

panna cotta surprise!

Create a sweet surprise inside a panna cotta by filling an individual cup or glass about half full with panna cotta. Chill for an hour, or until nearly set. Spoon in some fruit jam, or press a few berries into the soft pudding. Fill the glass the rest of the way with panna cotta and chill completely.

HOW DO YOU LIKE PANNA COTTA? TOTALLY SMOOTH OR A LITTLE CHUNKY?

People can have strong opinions about pudding. Some like it perfectly smooth, while others don't mind some chunky bits of fruit or nuts. If you're among the latter, stir fresh blueberries and chopped almonds into a batch of panna cotta and let it set. Or try it with strawberries and peaches, or chocolate shavings for a take on *straciatella*, the fabulous Italian ice cream streaked with chocolate.

COFFEE PANNA COTTA

Strong, hot, complex coffee is the first thing I taste every morning. I drink coffee not just because it is an efficient caffeine delivery system, but because I love the taste. I love the floral, winey notes of coffees from Ethiopia and the bittersweet caramel flavors of those from Guatemala. This panna cotta is perhaps the perfect dessert if, like me, you love the taste of coffee. It's pure; the coffee is steeped directly in the dairy and fills the mouth with its rich, roasted flavor.

MAKES SIX ½-CUP (120-ML) SERVINGS. GLUTEN-FREE.

- 1½ cups (360 ml) reduced-fat (2%) or whole milk
- 2¼ teaspoons powdered gelatin
- ⅓ cup (65 g) sugar
- 1½ cups (360 ml) cream
- ¼ cup (21 g) dark roasted coffee beans, ground extremely coarsely
- Pinch salt
- ¼ teaspoon pure vanilla extract

Pour the milk into a wide, shallow bowl and sprinkle the gelatin over the top. Set aside for 5 minutes to allow the gelatin to soften. Stir the sugar into the cream in a 2-quart (2-L) or larger saucepan. Bring to a simmer over medium heat, then whisk in the milk and gelatin. Whisk thoroughly over low heat until the gelatin has completely dissolved. Turn off the heat and stir in the coffee beans, salt, and vanilla. Steep for 5 minutes, then strain the panna cotta through a very fine-mesh sieve.

Divide this mixture among six ramekins or dessert glasses. Cover the glasses lightly with plastic wrap. Refrigerate the panna cotta and let it set for at least 2 hours—but preferably overnight, especially if you plan to unmold it. (If so, see the instructions on page 102.) The panna cotta can be made up to 3 days ahead and stored, covered, in the refrigerator.

MILKY CHOCOLATE PANNA COTTA

This panna cotta is soft and smooth—it tastes of milk, chocolate, and vanilla. It's rich without being overpowering, and it's easy to make and unmold, given the high ratio of real chocolate in the pudding.

MAKES SIX ½-CUP (120-ML) SERVINGS. GLUTEN-FREE.

- ¾ cup (180 ml) whole milk
- 1 teaspoon powdered gelatin
- 7 ounces (200 g) good-quality milk chocolate (such as Scharffen Berger), finely chopped
- 1¼ cups (300 ml) cream
- ¼ cup (50 g) sugar
- ¼ teaspoon salt
- ½ teaspoon pure vanilla extract

Pour the milk into a wide, shallow bowl and sprinkle the gelatin over the top. Set aside for 5 minutes to allow the gelatin to soften. Melt the chocolate carefully in a heavy 2-quart (2-L) saucepan set directly over medium-low heat, stirring frequently to ensure it does not scorch. When the chocolate is melted and smooth, gradually whisk in the cream. Whisk until smoothly incorporated, and continue heating until the cream is warm. Whisk in the sugar and the milk with the gelatin. Warm, whisking constantly, until the gelatin and sugar are dissolved and the mixture is perfectly smooth. Turn off the heat and whisk in the vanilla and salt.

Divide this mixture between six ramekins or dessert glasses. It is important to cover the chocolate mixture with plastic wrap or wax paper nearly touching the surface; otherwise, an extra-thick chocolate pudding skin will form. Refrigerate the panna cotta and let it set for at least 2 hours—but preferably overnight, especially if you plan to unmold it. (If so, see the instructions on page 102.) The panna cotta can be made up to 3 days ahead and stored, covered, in the refrigerator.

GRAPEFRUIT AND VANILLA BEAN PANNA COTTA

I feel like it's only fair for me to warn you about this panna cotta. It's not for everyone. The first taste brings a powerful intensity of grapefruit flavor—tart and more than a little bitter—followed by the smooth, sweet, vanilla-scented cream. For me, this marriage of tart and sweet, bitter and smooth, is completely addictive. My friend Devon, a wonderful pastry chef, taught me that not all panna cotta has to be made of milk and cream. You can replace some of the dairy in a panna cotta with fruit juice for a lighter, fresher taste and texture, as I do here. Be sure to use a grapefruit juice with no added sugar or flavorings. If you would prefer another flavor, nearly any juice will do—apple, grape, cranberry—you can even use iced green tea.

MAKES SIX ½-CUP (120-ML) SERVINGS. GLUTEN-FREE.

- 1½ cups (360 ml) pulp-free pink grapefruit juice
- 2¼ teaspoons powdered gelatin
- 1½ cups (360 ml) cream
- 6 tablespoons sugar (75 g), or to taste
- 1 vanilla bean, or 2 teaspoons pure vanilla extract
- Pinch salt
- ⅛ teaspoon ground ginger
- Fresh grapefruit segments, to serve
- Mint sprigs, to serve

Pour the grapefruit juice into a small saucepan and sprinkle the gelatin over the top. Set the pan aside for 5 minutes to allow the gelatin to soften. Warm it gently over medium heat, stirring constantly, until the gelatin is fully dissolved.

Warm the cream and sugar in a separate saucepan over medium heat. If you're using the vanilla bean, split it and scrape the seeds into the pan (see Note, page 33). Whisk the mixture so the seeds are incorporated into the liquid. When the vanilla bean has been scraped out, drop the entire pod into the cream as well. Turn off the heat. Let the mixture steep for 5 minutes.

Whisk in the grapefruit juice and gelatin. Taste to check sweetness; if necessary, add more sugar. Stir in the salt, ginger, and vanilla extract, if you did not use the whole bean. Whisk vigorously, then remove the vanilla bean pod.

Divide this mixture among six ramekins or dessert glasses. Cover the glasses lightly with plastic wrap. Refrigerate the panna cotta and let it set for at least 2 hours—but preferably overnight, especially if you plan to unmold it. (If so, see the instructions on page 102.) The panna cotta can be made up to 3 days ahead and stored, covered, in the refrigerator. Garnish each serving with a peeled segment of grapefruit and a short sprig of mint.

PEACH AND BUTTERMILK PANNA COTTA

I love buttermilk in panna cotta. Its tangy taste lightens the richness of the cream, making the pudding just a little more multidimensional. This is also a panna cotta that takes advantage of fresh fruit, with chunks of summer peach at the bottom of the glass. Dip your spoon down through the tangy pudding to find a big spoonful of golden summer fruit.

MAKES SIX ½-CUP (120-ML) SERVINGS. GLUTEN-FREE.

12 ounces (340 g) fresh peaches (2 large), peeled and finely chopped

1½ cups (360 ml) cultured buttermilk, well shaken, divided

2¼ teaspoons powdered gelatin

¼ cup (50 g) sugar, or to taste

1½ cups (360 ml) cream

1 teaspoon pure vanilla extract

⅛ teaspoon ground cloves

Pinch salt

Divide the peaches among six cups or glasses that hold at least 6 ounces (180 ml) each. Chill the glasses.

Pour ½ cup (120 ml) of the buttermilk into a 2-quart (2-L) saucepan and sprinkle the gelatin over the top. Set aside for 5 minutes to allow the gelatin to soften. Warm gently over medium heat and stir the sugar in. Heat gently until the gelatin and sugar have both fully dissolved, then turn off the heat.

Whisk in the remaining buttermilk and the cream, vanilla, cloves, and salt. Taste to check sweetness; add more sugar if desired.

Divide this mixture among the chilled cups, pouring it over the peaches. Cover the glasses lightly with plastic wrap. Refrigerate the panna cotta and let it set for at least 2 hours—but preferably overnight. The panna cotta can be made up to 3 days ahead and left in the refrigerator, covered.

SOUR CREAM PANNA COTTA
WITH CLEMENTINE CURD

Panna cotta can be made with nearly any combination of dairy products—and I especially like the tangy ones like buttermilk and yogurt. But my favorite panna cotta of all is made with sour cream. I use a little less gelatin than usual in these soft, velvety cups of pudding, tangy and bright from the sour cream and sweetened up with a topping of bright orange clementine curd.

MAKES SIX ½-CUP (120-ML) SERVINGS. GLUTEN-FREE.

1½ cups (360 ml) whole milk, divided

2 teaspoons powdered gelatin

6 tablespoons (75 g) sugar

1½ cups (360 ml) light or full-fat sour cream

1 teaspoon pure vanilla extract

Pinch salt

Clementine Curd to serve (page 172)

Orange peel twists, to garnish

Pour ½ cup (120 ml) of the milk into a small saucepan and sprinkle the gelatin over the top. Set aside for 5 minutes to allow the gelatin to soften. Warm the mixture gently over medium heat, stirring constantly, until the gelatin is fully dissolved. Whisk in the sugar and continue warming until the sugar is completely dissolved as well. Turn off the heat.

Whisk in the remaining milk and the sour cream, vanilla, and salt. Divide this mixture among six ramekins or dessert glasses. Cover the glasses lightly with plastic wrap. Refrigerate the panna cotta and let it set for at least 2 hours—but preferably overnight. The panna cotta can be made up to 3 days ahead and stored, covered, in the refrigerator.

To serve, top each cup of panna cotta with clementine curd and a twist of orange peel.

// PEACH AND BUTTERMILK PANNA COTTA

STRAWBERRY-YOGURT PANNA COTTA

Yogurt is a delicious substitute for milk in nearly any panna cotta recipe, but especially in this one, where the whole dish is lightened up with pureed strawberries, and the yogurt replaces a portion of the cream as well as the milk. It's tangy and sweet, with the true fragrance of summer strawberries.

MAKES SIX ½-CUP (120-ML) SERVINGS. GLUTEN-FREE.

- **4 cups (566 g) roughly chopped fresh strawberries**
- **2¼ teaspoons powdered gelatin**
- **1 cup (240 ml) cream**
- **¼ cup (50 g) sugar, or to taste**
- **½ cup (120 ml) plain full-fat yogurt**
- **¼ teaspoon rosewater (optional; see Note, page 55)**
- **Pinch salt**
- **Strawberry slices, to serve**

Puree the strawberries in a blender or food processor and pour them through a fine-mesh sieve. You should be left with approximately 1½ cups (360 ml) liquid. Sprinkle the gelatin over this strawberry juice in a wide, shallow bowl. Set aside for 5 minutes to allow the gelatin to soften.

Warm the cream and sugar in a 2-quart (2-L) or larger saucepan. Bring to a simmer over medium heat, then turn down the heat and whisk in the strawberry juice and gelatin. Whisk thoroughly over low heat until the gelatin has completely dissolved. Taste to check sweetness; if necessary, add more sugar. Turn off the heat and whisk in the yogurt, rosewater, if using, and salt.

Divide this mixture among six ramekins or dessert glasses. Cover the glasses lightly with plastic wrap. Refrigerate the panna cotta and let it set for at least 2 hours—but preferably overnight, especially if you plan to unmold it. (If so, see the instructions on page 102.) The panna cotta can be made up to 3 days ahead and stored, covered, in the refrigerator. Serve garnished with strawberry slices.

GOAT CHEESE PANNA COTTA
WITH CRANBERRY-PORT GLAZE

Like yogurt, goat cheese adds depth and tang to a panna cotta. I have even made savory goat cheese panna cottas as little bites to start a meal. This one is sweet, but mildly so, and it's topped with a festive layer of scarlet cranberry jelly. Serve this in clear glasses so your guests can admire the pretty contrast. It makes a great finish to a winter holiday meal.

You can also make the goat cheese panna cotta alone and serve it with something else; it's especially good with the gingery plum conserve on page 82.

MAKES SIX ½-CUP (120-ML) SERVINGS. GLUTEN-FREE.

for the panna cotta

- 8 ounces (225 g) goat cheese, softened
- 2 teaspoons powdered gelatin
- 2 cups (480 ml) whole milk, divided
- ⅓ cup (65 g) sugar, or to taste
- ⅛ teaspoon cardamom powder
- ¼ teaspoon cinnamon
- Pinch salt

for the cranberry-port glaze

- 2 (12-ounce / 340-g) bags fresh cranberries
- 1¼ cups (250 g) sugar
- ½ cup (120 ml) ruby port
- 1 long sprig rosemary
- 2½ teaspoons powdered gelatin

Chop or finely crumble the goat cheese into a bowl and set it aside. Sprinkle the gelatin over ½ cup (120 ml) of the milk in a wide, shallow bowl and set it aside to soften for 5 minutes.

Warm the remaining 1½ cups (360 ml) milk and the sugar in a 2-quart (2-L) saucepan over medium-high heat until small bubbles form around the edges. Whisk in the goat cheese and keep stirring until it melts. Add the milk and gelatin. Whisk vigorously until the gelatin and any remaining bits of goat cheese are thoroughly melted. Turn off the heat and stir in the cardamom, cinnamon, and salt.

Divide the panna cotta among six dessert glasses and put them in the refrigerator to chill while you make the cranberry layer.

Heat the cranberries with the sugar, 1 cup (240 ml) water, the port, and rosemary sprig in a 2-quart (2-L) saucepan over medium-high heat. Bring to a simmer and cook for 15 minutes, or until all the cranberries have burst open. Strain the liquid by pouring the mixture through a fine-mesh sieve, pressing on the cranberries to squeeze out as much as possible. You should have approximately 1½ cups (360 ml) liquid. Discard the cranberry solids. Sprinkle the gelatin over the liquid and let it sit for 5 minutes to soften. Pour the cranberry liquid back into the saucepan and heat it, stirring frequently, until the gelatin is fully dissolved. Turn off the heat and let the cranberry mixture cool for 15 to 30 minutes.

Evenly divide the cranberry mixture among the panna cotta glasses, which by now should be lightly set. Chill for at least 2 hours—but preferably overnight.

PINEAPPLE, VANILLA, AND COCONUT MILK PANNA COTTA

Panna cotta is a great dessert choice if you are avoiding dairy altogether. This is a basic recipe for a version made completely with full-fat coconut milk. Combined with pineapple juice, it's tropical and sunny! Look for coconut milk that has not been stabilized with guar gum. My favorite brands are Thai, especially Chaokoh.

MAKES SIX ½-CUP (120-ML) SERVINGS. GLUTEN-FREE. DAIRY-FREE.

- 1¼ cups (300 ml) chilled pineapple juice (see Note)
- 2¼ teaspoons powdered gelatin
- ¼ cup (50 g) sugar
- 1 (13.5-ounce / 400-ml) can coconut milk
- 1 vanilla bean
- Pinch salt
- 1 tablespoon rum (optional)

Pour the juice into a 2-quart (2-L) saucepan and sprinkle the gelatin over the top. Set aside for 5 minutes to allow the gelatin to soften. Warm the mixture over low heat and stir until the gelatin has dissolved.

Warm the coconut milk with the sugar in a separate saucepan over medium heat. While it is warming, split the vanilla bean and scrape the seeds into the pan (see Note, page 33). Whisk the mixture so the seeds are incorporated into the liquid. When the vanilla bean has been scraped out, drop the entire pod into the coconut milk as well. Turn off the heat. Let the mixture steep for 5 minutes. Remove the pod and discard.

Whisk the coconut milk into the juice and gelatin mixture, and whisk in the salt and rum, if using.

Divide this mixture among six ramekins or dessert glasses. Cover the glasses lightly with plastic wrap. Refrigerate the panna cotta and let it set for at least 2 hours—but preferably overnight, especially if you plan to unmold it. (If so, see the instructions on page 102.) The panna cotta can be made up to 3 days ahead and stored, covered, in the refrigerator.

NOTE // Make sure the pineapple juice has been pasteurized; if in doubt, heat the juice and let it simmer for 5 minutes. Chill the juice before proceeding. Unpasteurized pineapple juice has an enzyme that will destroy gelatin's thickening power.

ALMOND-AMARETTO PANNA COTTA

This dairy-free dessert embraces the sweet, nutty taste of almond milk. It's also more delicate and lower in fat than most panna cottas. I picked up a hint for this recipe from Hélène Dujardin at the lovely blog Tartelette (tarteletteblog.com)—she uses dairy-free creamer in her vegan panna cotta to make it richer. I used a vegan soy creamer, and I recommend using one without any added flavor or extra sweetener.

MAKES SIX ½-CUP (120-ML) SERVINGS. GLUTEN-FREE. DAIRY-FREE.

- 2 cups (480 ml) almond milk, divided
- 2½ teaspoons powdered gelatin
- 3 tablespoons sugar, or to taste
- 1 cup (240 ml) nondairy creamer
- 2 tablespoons amaretto liqueur, or ½ teaspoon almond extract
- 1 teaspoon pure vanilla extract
- ¼ teaspoon salt

Pour ½ cup (120 ml) of the almond milk into a wide, shallow bowl and sprinkle the gelatin over the top. Set aside for 5 minutes to allow the gelatin to soften. Warm over low heat and stir in the sugar. Warm gently until the sugar and gelatin have both completely dissolved. Turn off the heat.

Whisk in the remaining milk and the creamer, amaretto, vanilla, and salt. Taste to check sweetness; add more sugar if desired.

Divide this mixture among six ramekins or dessert glasses. Cover the glasses lightly with plastic wrap. Refrigerate the panna cotta and let it set for at least 2 hours—but preferably overnight, especially if you plan to unmold it. (If so, see the instructions on page 102.) The panna cotta can be made up to 3 days ahead and stored, covered, in the refrigerator.

EASY FLAVOR VARIATION
almond-amaretto panna cotta with brandied cherries

Spoon about ¼ cup (60 ml) Brandied Cherry Sauce (page 66) into the bottom of each of your serving glasses. Pour the panna cotta over the cherries and let set. (To help preserve the discrete layers, chill the cherries in the glasses for an hour before pouring in the panna cotta.)

YOGURT PUDDING SQUARES
WITH RASPBERRY-ANISE JELLY

These are soft squares—almost like a curd, wobbly and delicate in the mouth, with a bright pink layer of raspberry jelly on top. I love the aromatic taste of anise with the raspberry.

MAKES ABOUT 30 SMALL SQUARES. GLUTEN-FREE.

for the yogurt pudding squares

- **4** tablespoons (35 g) powdered gelatin
- **1** (14-ounce / 397-g) can sweetened condensed milk
- **3** cups (720 ml) plain, whole-milk yogurt
- **1** teaspoon pure vanilla extract
- **¼** teaspoon salt

for the raspberry-anise jelly

- **10** ounces (280 g) raspberries, fresh or frozen
- **2** pods star anise, broken into pieces
- **½** lemon, juiced (about 1 tablespoon)
- **1** cup (200 g) sugar
- **2** teaspoons powdered gelatin

Sprinkle the gelatin over 1 cup (240 ml) water in a 3-quart (2.8-L) or larger saucepan and allow the gelatin to soften for 5 minutes. Warm the pan over low heat until the gelatin has completely dissolved. Whisk in the condensed milk and continue warming until it is completely combined with the water. Turn off the heat. Whisk in 2 cups (480 ml) water and the yogurt. Whisk until well combined, and stir in the vanilla and salt. Pour into a 9-by-13-inch (23-by-33-cm) dish and refrigerate until set, about 2 hours.

Meanwhile, make the jelly. Cook the raspberries with the star anise, lemon juice, and 2 cups (480 ml) water for about 10 minutes, until the berries are extremely soft. Strain the mixture through a fine-mesh sieve, pushing on the raspberries to make them release their juices. Discard the solids and return the juice to the pan. Add the sugar and bring to a boil, stirring until it dissolves. Boil for 5 minutes, or until slightly reduced. Measure the jelly; you should have about 2 cups (480 ml).

In a separate small saucepan, sprinkle the gelatin over ¼ cup (60 ml) cold water and allow the gelatin to soften for 5 minutes. Warm the mixture over low heat, stirring frequently, until the gelatin dissolves. Whisk this into the warm raspberry jelly until fully incorporated. Pour the jelly into a large measuring cup or a bowl and set it aside to cool for at least 15 minutes.

Take the dish from the refrigerator and gently pour the raspberry jelly over the yogurt in an even layer. Return the dish to the refrigerator and chill it for an additional 2 to 4 hours, until the dessert is softly set. To serve, slice it into bars.

WHIPPED CLOUD PUDDING
(CREAMY BLANCMANGE)

Blancmange is one of the very oldest puddings, dating back to ancient times, when it was thickened with chicken, almonds, or rice (see more about this curious chicken pudding on page 33). It evolved into a simple milk pudding flavored with almonds and thickened with cornstarch or gelatin, a food that was considered to be very good for invalids.

This soft, cloudlike version of blancmange is not necessarily a recovery dish—it's enriched with whipped cream for a thick, creamy final texture, more luxurious than a simple panna cotta. It pays homage to its roots with a dash of almond-amaretto flavor.

MAKES 3 CUPS (720 ML) OR SIX SERVINGS. GLUTEN-FREE.

- 1½ cups (360 ml) whole milk, divided
- 2 teaspoons powdered gelatin
- ½ cup (100 g) sugar
- 1 tablespoon amaretto, or an extra ½ teaspoon almond extract
- 1 teaspoon pure vanilla extract
- ¼ teaspoon almond extract
  Pinch salt
- 1½ cups (360 ml) cream

Pour ½ cup (120 ml) of the milk into a small saucepan and sprinkle the gelatin over its surface. Let the gelatin soften for 5 minutes. Warm the milk gently over low heat, stirring frequently, until the gelatin is fully dissolved. Add the sugar and continue to heat for a few minutes more, stirring until it is also dissolved. Turn off the heat and stir in the rest of the milk, the amaretto, vanilla, almond extract, and salt.

In the bowl of a stand mixer (or in a large bowl with a hand mixer), whip the cream until it holds soft peaks. Gently fold in the milk and gelatin mixture. It will be liquidy with lumps of whipped cream. Divide this among six small cups or pour it into a 1-quart (1-L) dish and chill, lightly covered, for 2 to 4 hours, until softly set. To serve, spoon into small dishes.

BREAKFAST YOGURT PARFAIT
WITH GRANOLA AND JAM

Pudding for breakfast! Well, not quite. This yogurt parfait has less sugar than the average pudding, and it's not as firmly set, but it's a good way to prepare a yogurt parfait ahead of time, since using a little bit of gelatin helps the yogurt stay firm and not release water. It also gives the yogurt a more luxurious mouthfeel. This is a great dish to offer at brunch or on a breakfast buffet.

MAKES 6 CUPS (1.4-L) OR SIX SERVINGS. GLUTEN-FREE.

- 2½ teaspoons powdered gelatin
- ¼ cup (60 ml) honey
- 1 cup (240 ml) cream, at room temperature
- 4 cups (960 ml) plain whole-milk or low-fat yogurt, at room temperature
- 1 cup (240 ml) berry jam, slightly warmed, divided
- 2 cups (245 g) granola, divided

Sprinkle the gelatin over ¼ cup (60 ml) water in a small saucepan and allow it to soften for 5 minutes. Warm the pan over medium heat, stirring frequently, just until the gelatin dissolves. Add the honey and continue stirring until the honey is combined with the gelatin and water. Whisk in the cream and turn off the heat.

In a large bowl, whisk together the honey and cream mixture with the yogurt. Spread half of this into a large glass serving bowl or trifle bowl. Pour half of the jam over the yogurt mixture and sprinkle with half of the granola. Repeat, adding the rest of the yogurt, then the jam, and topping with granola.

Refrigerate for several hours or overnight. Sprinkle with extra granola, if desired, to make sure the top is crunchy.

EASY FLAVOR VARIATION
fresh fruit yogurt parfait

You can skip the jam and use fresh fruit instead. Try berries, like strawberries and raspberries, or peeled peach slices. Be prepared for the fruit to sink into the yogurt a little bit, so the layers may not be very distinct. If you want firm layers, refrigerate the first layer of yogurt for 1 hour before adding the fruit and next layer of yogurt.

MOUSSE & BLENDER PUDDINGS

Mousse means "foam" in French, and the best mousse does indeed taste like airy foam. Unlike smooth, creamy custard and panna cotta, mousse dissolves on the tongue, light and full of tiny bubbles.

This delicate lightness is achieved in several ways, but traditionally mousse is whipped up with a combination of the techniques we've used separately in this book: Custard—made with egg yolks—is folded together with whipped cream and egg foam, and stabilized with gelatin.

There are other methods of making a light and creamy dessert, too, especially when working with chocolate. The first recipe here is perhaps the easiest one in the whole book: Whip eggs with melted chocolate and ta-da! Mousse! It doesn't even need gelatin. I offer several recipes for this and other quick, shortcut "blender" mousses.

But given that the other puddings in this collection are quite rich, this chapter concentrates on mousse recipes that contain egg whites. I like the light, almost crackly texture whipped egg whites add to a mousse.

ABOUT RAW EGGS

Many of the mousse recipes in this chapter use raw eggs or egg whites. If you are concerned about eating raw egg whites, I recommend purchasing pasteurized eggs or egg whites from your grocery store. (Use a pinch of cream of tartar when whipping these egg whites to make sure they whip up stiff enough. They will take much longer to whip than regular egg whites.)

Personally, I don't mind eating raw eggs from time to time. I buy organic, free-range eggs from a local farm, and I have never had a problem.

BASIC METHOD FOR CLASSIC MOUSSE

1 **Make a custard:** First, make a custard with egg yolks and cream or juice.
2 **Soften and dissolve the gelatin:** Soften the gelatin in a little bit of cold liquid, then dissolve in the warm custard.
3 **Whip the egg whites:** Whip the egg whites with sugar until firm and glossy.
4 **Whip the cream:** Whip the cream until it holds soft peaks.
5 **Fold it all together:** Fold all three components together and transfer to molds or a serving dish to chill for 1 to 3 hours, until softly set.

// DEEPEST CHOCOLATE MOUSSE

DEEPEST CHOCOLATE MOUSSE

If you want really intense chocolate pudding—deep, *dark* chocolate pudding—then start here. This comes together in just a few minutes, blending up in a flash. It's rich, a little boozy, with a touch of salt. It's the fastest way to a fantastic chocolate fix.

MAKES SIX ⅓-CUP (75-ML) SERVINGS. GLUTEN-FREE.

- ¾ **cup (180 ml) whole milk**
- ¼ **cup (60 ml) freshly brewed strong coffee**
- 6 **ounces (170 g) good-quality semisweet chocolate, finely chopped**
- 2 **eggs, lightly beaten**
- 2 **tablespoons dark rum (optional)**
- 1 **teaspoon pure vanilla extract**
- ¼ **teaspoon salt**
  Unsweetened whipped cream, to serve

In a small saucepan, warm the milk and coffee over medium heat until the mixture just comes to a simmer. Place the chocolate in a heatproof glass or metal mixing bowl and pour the milk and coffee mixture over it. Stir once, then let stand for 5 minutes.

Scrape the mixture into a blender and add the eggs, rum, vanilla, and salt. Blend until well combined. Pour into six small cups or a 1-quart (1-L) dish and chill for 2 hours, or until set. Serve with a dollop of unsweetened whipped cream.

CHOCOLATE-COCONUT MOUSSE

This is another dark, deep chocolate mousse—and it is completely vegan and dairy-free. This is a classic preparation in vegan circles, but whether you follow such a diet or not, you'll appreciate its light, silken texture and pure chocolate taste.

MAKES SIX ½-CUP (120-ML) SERVINGS. GLUTEN-FREE. DAIRY-FREE.

- ½ **cup (120 ml) coconut milk**
- 6 **ounces (170 g) bittersweet chocolate, finely chopped**
- 12 **ounces (340 g) soft or silken tofu**
- ¼ **cup (60 ml) Grade B maple syrup (see Note, page 62)**
- 1 **teaspoon pure vanilla extract**
- ¼ **teaspoon salt**
  Cinnamon, to serve

In a heavy saucepan, warm the coconut milk over medium heat until it comes to a simmer, then pour it over the chocolate in a heatproof glass or metal bowl. Stir once, then let stand for 5 minutes. Whisk until smooth.

Put the tofu, maple syrup, vanilla, and salt in a blender and whiz until smooth. Pour in the chocolate mixture and blend until smooth. Pour into six small cups or a 1-quart (1-L) dish and chill for 2 hours, or until set. Serve with a dusting of cinnamon.

EASY AND LIGHT PEACH BLENDER MOUSSE

This mousse skips the eggs and most of the dairy, for a simple, refreshing mousse that is one of the lightest, easiest recipes in this collection. It is inspired by Asian pudding recipes, using gelatin to thicken and adding just a smidge of cream for an extra boost of richness. It is also free of added sugar, with a mild sweetness that comes only from the peaches themselves.

Usually I prefer fresh fruit, when available, in mousse and pudding, but here I actually recommend canned peaches for convenience (no peeling!) and for their candied sweetness.

MAKES SIX ½-CUP (120-ML) SERVINGS. GLUTEN-FREE.

- 2 **(15-ounce / 425-g) cans peaches in juice (not syrup)**
- ½ **lemon, juiced (about 1½ tablespoons)**
- 3 **teaspoons powdered gelatin**
- ½ **cup (120 ml) cream**
- ¼ **teaspoon salt**
  Mint sprigs, to garnish

Drain the peaches and reserve ½ cup (120 ml) of the liquid. Put this liquid in a small saucepan with the lemon juice and sprinkle the gelatin over it. Set aside for 5 minutes to let the gelatin soften.

Blend the peaches, cream, and salt in a blender until smooth.

Warm the peach liquid over medium-low heat and stir until the gelatin dissolves. Pour this into the blender and blend for 1 minute more. Pour into six individual cups or a 1-quart (1-L) dish. Refrigerate 2 hours, or until set. Garnish with fresh sprigs of mint before serving.

EASY FLAVOR VARIATIONS
strawberry blender mousse

Substitute 3 heaping cups (about 425 g) chopped fresh, or frozen and thawed, strawberries for the peaches. Dissolve the gelatin in water or white grape juice instead of the peach juice.

mango blender mousse

Substitute 3 heaping cups fresh mango, from 3 to 4 large (about 340 g each) really, really ripe mangos (they should be very fragrant). Dissolve the gelatin in water or white grape juice instead of the peach juice.

WHITE CHOCOLATE MOUSSE

Your reaction to this creamy white chocolate mousse will probably depend on your feelings about white chocolate in general. Is it an oxymoron, a substance devoid of anything that actually makes chocolate *chocolate*? Or is white chocolate its own kind of pleasure, milky and creamy with cocoa butter? I espouse the latter opinion; I love the way the richness of white chocolate melts in the mouth. This recipe plays up the sweetness of white chocolate in a rich yet airy mousse.

MAKES SIX 1-CUP (240-ML) SERVINGS. GLUTEN-FREE.

1¼ **cups (300 ml) cream, divided**

7 **ounces (200 g) high-quality white chocolate, finely chopped**

1 **teaspoon powdered gelatin**

3 **large egg whites**

3 **tablespoons sugar**

1 **teaspoon pure vanilla extract**

⅛ **teaspoon salt**

Warm 1 cup (240 ml) of the cream over medium-high heat until it just begins to simmer. Pour this over the white chocolate in a heatproof bowl. Stir once, then let stand for 5 minutes.

Pour the remaining ¼ cup (60 ml) cream into a small saucepan and sprinkle the gelatin evenly over the surface. Set aside for 5 minutes for the gelatin to soften.

Add the egg whites to the bowl of a stand mixer (or use a large bowl and an electric hand mixer) and beat. When the whites turn foamy and opaque, gradually add the sugar and continue beating until they form soft yet glossy peaks. Set aside in a separate bowl.

Warm the cream and gelatin over medium-low heat, stirring until the granules are fully dissolved. Whisk this together with the cream and white chocolate, until the white chocolate has fully melted. Pour this into the mixer bowl and whip on medium speed for 5 minutes, or until the mixture is no longer hot but lukewarm. Beat in the vanilla and salt. Gently fold in the egg whites.

Spread the mousse in six separate cups or a 2-quart (2-L) dish and refrigerate for 2 hours, or until set.

CARDAMOM-YOGURT MOUSSE
WITH APRICOTS

This yogurt mousse is an exercise in nostalgia for me, evocative of two different memories. The first is recent: cold *lassi* spiked with cardamom, a favorite drink at Indian restaurants. The musky flavor of cardamom just plays well with the tangy, refreshing taste of yogurt. And so does honey, which brings me to my second memory. My mother often served me and my siblings big bowls of plain yogurt with honey swirled in—it was a favorite summer lunch. I remember how the honey laced the yogurt in thick ropes of sweetness. This is a plain yet comforting dish, the two flavors marrying perfectly.

I bring these three tastes together here in this dish, and finish it all off with fresh summer apricots. Top the finished mousse with apricot slices, or get fancy and pipe the chilled, set mousse into apricot halves and garnish with mint.

MAKES SIX ½-CUP (120-ML) SERVINGS. GLUTEN-FREE.

- 2 teaspoons powdered gelatin
- ⅓ cup (75 ml) honey
- 2 large egg whites
- ¾ cup (180 ml) cream
- 1½ cups (360 ml) plain Greek or strained yogurt (low-fat or full-fat)
- ½ teaspoon cardamom powder
- Pinch salt
- 6 to 8 ripe apricots, to serve

Pour ¼ cup (60 ml) water into a small saucepan and sprinkle the gelatin over it. Set aside for 5 minutes to allow the gelatin to soften. Set the pan over medium heat and whisk until the gelatin dissolves. Whisk in the honey and continue warming until the honey has thinned.

In the bowl of a stand mixer (or in a large bowl, using a hand mixer), whip the egg whites until stiff. Scrape out into a separate bowl. Wipe out the mixing bowl and beat the cream until stiff peaks form. Add the yogurt and whip until combined. Beat in the cardamom and salt, then slowly pour in the warmed honey and gelatin and whip. Use a spatula to gently fold in the egg whites.

Spread the mousse in six separate cups or in a 1-quart (1-L) dish and refrigerate for 1 to 2 hours, until softly set. Serve with slices of fresh apricot, or remove the pits from apricot halves and pipe in dollops of mousse.

CARA CARA ORANGE MOUSSE

This dessert is just like a Creamsicle—but all grown up; it's airy and rich at the same time. It calls for Cara Cara navel oranges, which are bright pink inside and have a more complex sweetness than most oranges. But you can use any other sort of orange citrus, like navel oranges, tangerines, or clementines—blood oranges would give this mousse a very pretty pinkish color, too. If you don't want to go to the bother of juicing oranges, you can just substitute plain orange juice (you'll still need one orange for the zest, though).

The method for this recipe involves a more traditional mousse preparation, creating a citrus custard, then folding it into whipped egg whites. (See Note, page 124 for information on using raw egg whites.) It's a sweet dessert for wintertime, when citrus is in season and a little extra sunshine is always welcome.

And, hey, a bonus: If you pour this finished mousse into molds (or pack it into a loaf pan) and freeze it, you really will have homemade Creamsicles. These taste like the real thing—but even better.

MAKES SIX 1-CUP (240-ML) SERVINGS. GLUTEN-FREE.

- 2 teaspoons powdered gelatin
- 4 Cara Cara navel oranges
- 4 tablespoons (56 g) unsalted butter
- ½ cup (100 g) sugar, divided
- 4 large eggs, separated
- ¾ cup (180 ml) cream
- 1 teaspoon pure vanilla extract
- ¼ teaspoon salt

Sprinkle the gelatin over ¼ cup (60 ml) water in a small saucepan and set aside for 5 minutes to allow the gelatin to soften.

Using a sharp vegetable peeler to avoid the pith, completely zest one of the oranges and set the zest aside. Take 6 long, curling strips of zest off the remaining oranges and set them aside for garnish. Juice the oranges and strain; you should have between ⅔ and ¾ cup (165 and 180 ml).

Melt the butter in a 2-quart (2-L) saucepan over medium heat; add in the orange juice and half of the sugar and stir until the sugar dissolves. In a separate small bowl, beat the egg yolks. Temper the egg yolks by pouring in a few spoonfuls of the warmed juice and whisking. Pour this back into the pan, whisking constantly, and cook for about 10 minutes, whisking frequently, until the curd thickens just slightly and coats the back of a spoon. Turn off the heat.

Warm the gelatin mixture over low heat until the granules have completely dissolved. Whisk this into the warm juice and egg-yolk mixture. Turn off the heat and set aside.

In the bowl of a stand mixer (or in a large bowl, using a hand mixer), whip the egg whites until stiff. Gradually add the remaining sugar in 1-tablespoon increments and beat until the egg whites are glossy and hold stiff peaks. Transfer them to a separate mixing bowl and set aside.

Wipe out the mixing bowl and add the cream, vanilla, and salt. Whip the cream until stiff peaks form. Fold this gently into the egg whites, then gently fold in the curd and the reserved orange zest.

Spread the mousse in six individual cups or in a 2-quart (1.89-L) serving dish (lightly greased, if you intend to unmold it). Refrigerate for 4 hours, or until completely set. Garnish with the reserved orange curls.

MELON-HONEY MOUSSE

The delicate taste of cantaloupe is one of my favorite summer flavors. This mousse spreads it through an airy, crinkly mass of sweetness—light as a cloud, and tasting of ripe summer fruit and honey.

MAKES EIGHT ½-CUP (120-ML) SERVINGS. GLUTEN-FREE.

1½ teaspoons powdered gelatin

1 lemon, juiced (about 3 tablespoons)

¼ cup (60 ml) honey

½ medium cantaloupe, peeled and diced (about 2 cups or 12 ounces / 340 grams)

½ cup (120 ml) plain full-fat yogurt

2 large egg whites

½ cup (120 ml) cream

¼ teaspoon salt

Sprinkle the gelatin over the lemon juice and 2 tablespoons water in a small saucepan, and let sit for 5 minutes to allow the gelatin to soften. Warm the pan over medium heat and stir until the gelatin is completely dissolved. Stir in the honey and continue warming until it is completely dissolved as well. Turn off the heat.

Blend the cantaloupe with the yogurt in a food processor or blender until very smooth. Pour the honey mixture into the melon mixture and blend.

In the bowl of a stand mixer (or in a large bowl, using a hand mixer), beat the egg whites until they hold soft peaks. Transfer these to a separate bowl. Wipe out the mixer bowl and add the cream. Beat until it holds firm peaks.

Gently fold all three together—the melon mixture, egg whites, and cream—and stir in the salt. Spread the mousse (it will be quite thin and liquid) in eight separate cups or in a 1-quart (1-L) dish and refrigerate for 2 hours, or until softly set.

COCONUT-RICOTTA MOUSSE
WITH PISTACHIO AND POMEGRANATE

Ricotta makes a particularly rich and luxurious style of mousse, thicker than ones lightened with egg whites. This is a beautiful dessert when you garnish with pistachios and pomegranate seeds (called arils). White, green, and red—festive, delicious, and just a little different.

1½ cups (360 ml) cream, divided

2½ teaspoons powdered gelatin

8 ounces (225 g) full-fat ricotta cheese

½ cup (120 ml) coconut cream (the thickest cream from the top of the can of milk)

¼ cup (50 g) sugar

1 teaspoon pure vanilla extract

¼ teaspoon ground ginger

¼ teaspoon salt

½ cup (62 g) pistachio nutmeats, to serve

½ cup (87 g) pomegranate arils, to serve

Pour ½ cup (120 ml) of the cream into a small saucepan and sprinkle the gelatin on top. Set aside for 5 minutes to allow the gelatin to soften. Warm the pan over medium heat and whisk until the gelatin dissolves.

Whip the ricotta and coconut cream together in the bowl of a stand mixer (or in a large bowl, using a hand mixer). Add the remaining cream and continue beating until the mixture forms soft peaks. Slowly add the sugar, 1 tablespoon at a time. Beat in the warm cream-gelatin mixture, the vanilla, ginger, and salt.

Spread in a 1-quart (1-L) dish and refrigerate for 2 hours, or until set. Scoop out in fluffy spoonfuls into dessert glasses. Serve garnished with the pistachios and pomegranate arils.

5 REAL FRUIT JELLIES

Wiggly, jiggly, sweet, and shiny! Kids love jelled desserts, and I admit to still loving them, too. What I don't love are the fake, artificially colored powders out of a box. Lime Jell-O? I admire its shocking bright green color, but it doesn't taste like any lime that ever came off a tree.

The good news is that you can easily make "Jell-O" from any fruit juice, using only plain, sugar-free gelatin to set the juice into a firm consistency. It literally takes five minutes of hands-on time, and you don't even need to add extra sugar. (For general instructions and tips about gelatin, as well as vegetarian substitutes, refer back to chapter 3, pages 94–121.)

This chapter contains instructions for making wobbly or firm fruit jellies out of natural, unsweetened fruit juice, along with other creative ideas for cooking up jellies for dessert. As I stated earlier, this book is focused on sweets that make a satisfying end to a meal—not just little snacks. So this chapter focuses on light, refreshing sweets to close a meal: squares of jelly skewered with herbs, ready to be dipped in whipped cream; striped jelly terrines (so pretty!); and some inside-out fruit surprises.

I do keep things fairly simple in this chapter, however; while I love retro jelly molds and terrines, I think my favorite jelly desserts are the plainest ones—apple or orange juice jelled into a soft spoonful through the alchemy of gelatin. All the desserts in this chapter lean toward the natural, the unadorned, letting fruit and its juicy flavor speak for themselves.

Here are two different sets of instructions for making fruit jelly: Which one you use depends on how firm you want the jelly to be. The first sets the jelly to a solid yet wobbly consistency. It's best left in the dish and eaten with a spoon. The second sets up much firmer, so it can be unmolded or cut out with cookie cutters into fun, jiggly shapes.

SOFTER JELLY TO EAT WITH A SPOON

This jelly sets firm but not quite firm enough to unmold cleanly. It's best poured into individual cups, or into a big dish, for scooping out in thick, wobbly spoonfuls. As with a pudding, the shallower the dish, the faster this will chill and set. If you're in a hurry, pour it into a 9-by-13-inch (23-by-33-cm) baking pan. But do not freeze it—that will destroy the gelatin's setting power.

MAKES SIX ½-CUP (120-ML) SERVINGS. GLUTEN-FREE. DAIRY-FREE.

3 **cups (720 ml) fruit juice such as apple, grape, orange, or a combination, divided**

3 **teaspoons powdered gelatin**

Pour ½ cup (120 ml) of the fruit juice into a small, wide saucepan. Sprinkle the gelatin over the fruit juice and set aside for about 5 minutes. The gelatin will soften and wrinkle. Put the saucepan over low heat and warm the liquid, whisking frequently, for about 5 minutes, or until the gelatin dissolves completely. Lift the whisk or tilt the pan to wash the liquid up the sides; if you see small grains of undissolved gelatin, it isn't done yet. Do not boil the mixture, just warm it gently.

Add the rest of the juice and whisk to combine. Divide the mixture among six ½-cup (120-ml) cups or pour it into a 1-quart (1-L) dish. Refrigerate for 2 hours, or until softly set.

FIRM FRUIT JELLY TO UNMOLD OR FOR CUTOUTS

This jelly is not as delicate—you can unmold it or chill it in a shallow sheet pan and use cookie cutters to make jiggly cutouts, like the Jell-O Jigglers of our youth.

MAKES SIX ½-CUP (120-ML) SERVINGS. GLUTEN-FREE. DAIRY-FREE.

- 3 **cups (720 ml) fruit juice such as apple, grape, orange, or a combination, divided**
- 6 **teaspoons powdered gelatin**

Pour 1 cup (240 ml) of the fruit juice into a small, wide saucepan. Sprinkle the gelatin over the fruit juice and set aside for about 5 minutes. The gelatin will soften and wrinkle. Put the saucepan over low heat and warm the liquid, whisking frequently, for about 5 minutes, or until the gelatin dissolves completely. Lift the whisk or tilt the pan to wash the liquid up the sides; if you see small grains of undissolved gelatin, it isn't done yet. Do not boil the mixture, just warm it gently.

Add the rest of the juice and whisk to combine. Divide the mixture among six ½-cup (120-ml) molds or pour it into a 1-quart (1-L) dish. If you want to make thinner cutouts, pour it into a 9-inch (23-cm) square baking dish. Refrigerate for 4 hours or overnight, until firmly set. Unmold (see sidebar, below) and use small cookie cutters to cut shapes out of the gelatin, if desired.

TIPS FOR UNMOLDING JELLIES

Molded jellies are pure fun—colorful and quivering, they look delicious and alien at the same time, and honestly, people can't resist them. It's not difficult to unmold a jelly from a pan or a cup; in fact, I find it rather easier than taking a cake out of a pan in one piece. Here are some practical tips for making your jellies slide right out.

1 To prepare a mold or a cup, lightly moisten a paper towel with neutral-flavored vegetable oil. Wipe the inside of the mold with the paper towel. Then wipe it down again with a dry, clean paper towel, leaving only the faintest residue of oil behind.

2 Chill the oiled mold before pouring in the jelly mixture.

3 Once you've poured the mixture in, chill it at least overnight.

4 To unmold, fill a large bowl or stockpot about three-quarters full with warm water. Carefully lower the mold into the warm water, just until the water reaches the rim. Watch the surface of the jelly and look for the top edge to start loosening from the side of the mold or cup. This will take anywhere from 30 seconds to 2 minutes, depending on the size of the mold, the temperature of the water, and how long the mold has been chilled.

5 Lightly wet the serving plate before turning the jelly out on it. This will let you reposition the jelly to just the right spot on the plate or platter.

6 If necessary, use a flexible knife to gently help the edges loosen. Then turn the jelly out quickly and carefully onto a platter. If it doesn't release immediately, return the mold to the warm water bath for another 15 seconds.

LAYERING JELLIES

There are several recipes in this chapter that direct you to layer different flavors of jelly or milk jelly for pretty terrines. Here are some general instructions and tips for doing so successfully.

1 Freeze the container or loaf pan so it is really chilled before you begin to layer.

2 Pour in the first layer and let it chill until nearly firm.

3 When pouring the next layer of jelly over the first, the liquid should be lukewarm at most, not hot. Use a back-and-forth pouring motion, or a circular motion, so the stream doesn't melt through the first layer.

4 Chill each layer of jelly for 30 to 60 minutes, depending on the thickness of the layer and size of the dish. The layer should be relatively firm, but it will still stick to your finger when lightly pressed.

EXPERT TIPS ON LAYERING AND UNMOLDING JELLIES FROM VICTORIA BELANGER

Victoria Belanger is the Jell-O Mold Mistress of Brooklyn (jellomoldmistress.com) and the author of *Hello, Jell-O!*, a bright and delicious little guidebook to gelatin desserts. She offers some tips here for making layered desserts and getting them out of the pan in one piece.

Layering Like a Pro

To create layers in a gelatin mold, refrigerate the first layer in the mold until it is nearly set, but still sticky to the touch. If one layer is too firm, the layer placed on top will slide right off. Conversely, if one layer is too soft, the colors will blend together. Make sure the gelatin mixture for the second layer has cooled before gently pouring it into the mold to avoid melting the first layer beneath.

Unmolding Like a Pro

Unmolding gelatin can seem like an impossible task, but with these simple steps it can be easy: Immerse the mold in warm water up to, but not over, the rim, keeping it submerged for 15 seconds. Moisten a serving plate (so you can slide your mold and center it on the plate once unmolded) and place it upside-down over the mold. Then hold the mold and the plate together, invert, and shake slightly to loosen the gelatin, carefully pulling the mold away.

AND A BONUS TIP: Victoria's favorite fruit juice for jellies is one you may not have thought of: pomegranate! It makes beautiful jellies, especially with fruit suspended inside.

JELLY TROUBLESHOOTING

Uh-oh . . . jelly not jelled? Here are a few troubleshooting questions for the one main problem you can have with gelatin: The jelly never got solid!

» **Dissolve!** Did you dissolve the gelatin completely so that no more grains could be seen in the liquid? Make sure the gelatin is *fully* dissolved.

» **Check the temperature:** Don't boil gelatin—boiling really messes with it. Also, did your jelly freeze inadvertently? Freezing destroys gelatin's thickening power.

» **Chill out!** Has the jelly been in the fridge long enough? Give it another hour or two and see how it looks.

» **Double-check your measurements:** Make sure you used the exact ratio of gelatin to liquid that was called for in the recipe.

» **Acidity:** Did you try to make jelly out of a high-acid fruit juice or soda pop? You may need a little extra gelatin.

SERVING IDEAS

Jelly gets a bad rap as a dessert. On the one hand, it's considered kid food, more suitable for after-school snacks than an elegant grown-up dinner. On the other hand, it can appear fussy and old-school—jelly molds? Who has one of *those* in the cupboard?

When served well, jelly can play both ways, and more. This chapter will show you it's not hard to make jelly desserts, and they can be lovely for dinner parties as well as snacks for kids.

Think about elegant toppings that you would use for other desserts and apply them to jelly: whipped cream, sprigs of herbs, chopped nuts, fruit sauce. Slice fruit jellies and use them as a base for one of the mousses in chapter 4, like Cara Cara Orange Mousse (page 132) on a bed of tangerine fruit jelly, or Cardamom-Yogurt Mousse (page 131) on a little raft of cherry jelly. Top finished jellies with chopped pistachios, or slice terrines of fruit and milk jelly and serve with fruit puree—jelly is for grown-ups too, kids!

APPLE-GINGER JELLY

In my family, a sick child was consoled with a bowl of quivering lime Jell-O and a glass of Gatorade, two such highly desirable foods in our household that certain children were known to exaggerate and downright lie about upset tummies, sore throats, and hot foreheads.

You don't need to be sick to enjoy this sparkling jelly, although it does include apple juice and ginger ale, two very good and gentle foods for someone getting over a sore throat. It has a mild sweetness and a bit of zip from the ginger ale. Pour this into little cups; it sets softly.

MAKES SIX ½-CUP (120-ML) SERVINGS. GLUTEN-FREE. DAIRY-FREE.

- 2 cups (480 ml) unsweetened apple juice or cider, divided
- 2½ teaspoons powdered gelatin
- 1 cup (240 ml) high-quality, spicy ginger ale, such as Fever-Tree or Q Ginger (see Sources, page 213)
  Whipped cream (page 167) or Cardamom-Yogurt Mousse (page 131, prepared without apricots), to serve (optional)

Pour ½ cup (120 ml) of the apple juice into a small saucepan and sprinkle the gelatin evenly over the surface. Set the pan aside to allow the gelatin to soften for 5 minutes.

Turn the heat on to low and slowly warm the mixture, whisking the gelatin until it is fully dissolved. Whisk in the remaining 1½ cups (360 ml) apple juice and the ginger ale and pour into six ½-cup (120-ml) cups, or into a 1-quart (1-L) dish. Refrigerate for 2 hours, or until softly set. (The gelatin will get firmer the longer it remains refrigerated.)

Serve with a dollop of whipped cream or cardamom-yogurt mousse, if desired.

FRESH WATERMELON-LIME JELLY

This is one of the most refreshing and delicious jellies I know. It has a gorgeous hot-pink color! This jelly is best made with only truly good and sweet watermelons, in high summer. The sugar amount is up to you; if you have a perfect watermelon, you may not need any at all.

MAKES SIX ½-CUP (120-ML) SERVINGS. GLUTEN-FREE. DAIRY-FREE.

- 3 pounds (1.4 kg) seedless watermelon
- 2 limes, juiced (about 1/4 cup / 60 ml)
- 3 teaspoons powdered gelatin
- 1 to 2 tablespoons sugar, or to taste

Peel and roughly cube the watermelon. Puree it thoroughly in a blender or food processor and pour it through a fine-mesh strainer. You should have approximately 3 cups (720 ml) liquid.

Combine 1 cup (240 ml) of the watermelon juice with the lime juice in a small saucepan and sprinkle the gelatin over its surface. Let the gelatin soften for 5 minutes, then warm the pan over medium heat, stirring frequently, until the gelatin is fully dissolved. Whisk the mixture together with the remaining watermelon juice. Taste, and add 1 to 2 tablespoons sugar if more sweetness is desired.

Pour into six ½-cup (120-ml) small cups or into a loaf pan and chill until set.

LEMONADE JELLY WITH BASIL

Lemon makes a tart, grown-up jelly, infused here with basil for an herbal aroma that sets off the summery sweetness. (Leave out the basil if you just want simple lemonade jelly.) One lemon tip, which I picked up from the Jellymongers themselves, Bompas & Parr (two young jelly-obsessed Brits who have filled rooms with alcoholic mists and created models of architectural monuments out of fruit gelatin): Adding a bit of orange juice turns otherwise pale lemon jelly into exactly the bright yellow you would expect from its tart, sunny taste.

MAKES SIX 1/2-CUP (120-ML) SERVINGS. GLUTEN-FREE. DAIRY-FREE.

- **4 to 5 large lemons, juiced (3/4 cup / 180 ml)**
- **3/4 cup (150 g) sugar**
- **1 1/2 cups (25 g) loosely packed basil leaves, plus more to serve**
- **1/2 cup (120 ml) pulp-free orange juice**
- **3 teaspoons powdered gelatin**
- **Whipped cream (see page 167), to serve**

Warm the lemon juice, 1 1/2 cups (360 ml) water, and the sugar to boiling. Stir until the sugar is completely dissolved. Roughly tear the basil leaves and put them in a small bowl. Pour the lemon juice mixture over the basil leaves and let steep for at least 15 minutes.

Pour the orange juice into a small saucepan and sprinkle the gelatin over its surface. Let the gelatin soften for 5 minutes, then warm the pan over medium heat, stirring frequently, until the gelatin is fully dissolved. Turn off the heat.

Strain the basil out of the lemon juice and whisk the juice into the gelatin mixture. Pour the liquid into six small cups or a 1-quart (1-L) dish. Refrigerate for 2 hours, or until softly set. Garnish with whipped cream and basil leaves to serve.

LEMON-BASIL JELLY SKEWERS

To make little bites for a party, double the amount of gelatin in this recipe to 6 full teaspoons. Pour the mixture into an 8- or 9-inch (20- or 23-cm) square baking dish and let it set overnight in the refrigerator. Cut it into 1-inch (2.5-cm) squares, or use a small cookie cutter to cut out 1-inch (2.5-cm) circles. Skewer one or two pieces on a toothpick or party pick with a leaf of fresh basil folded and skewered at one end. Chill until ready to serve, and pass a bowl of whipped cream for dipping.

EASY FLAVOR VARIATIONS
real lime jelly

For real lime jelly (with the taste of fresh limes and no nasty green food coloring), substitute juice from 7 to 8 limes for the lemon juice. Substitute water for the orange juice.

meyer lemon jelly with lavender

Extra-sweet, less acidic Meyer lemons are also wonderful in this jelly, especially with the herbal-floral taste of lavender. Simply substitute Meyers for the regular lemons. You may need one or two extra lemons, as Meyer lemons are generally smaller. Instead of steeping basil in the juice, steep 1 tablespoon dried food-grade lavender buds. Strain after 10 minutes and proceed as directed above.

WHITE GRAPE AND ELDERFLOWER JELLY
WITH BLACKBERRIES

This sweet jelly depends on the fragrant taste of elderflower syrup, perhaps most commonly found in the food section at your local IKEA store, or online (see Sources, page 213).

MAKES 3 CUPS (720 ML) OR
SIX SERVINGS. GLUTEN-FREE.
DAIRY-FREE.

- **1 lemon, zested and juiced (about 3 tablespoons)**
- **3 teaspoons powdered gelatin**
- **2 cups (480 ml) white grape juice, at room temperature**
- **¾ cup (180 ml) elderflower syrup, at room temperature**
- **1 cup (144 g) whole fresh blackberries**

Mix the lemon juice and ½ cup (120 ml) water in a small saucepan. Sprinkle the gelatin over the surface and let it soften for 5 minutes. Turn the heat on to medium-low and warm the liquid until the gelatin has fully dissolved.

Whisk in the grape juice, syrup, and lemon zest. Pour into a 2-quart (2-L) dish, such as an 8-inch (20-cm) square baking pan. Set in the fridge on a level surface and chill for 30 minutes. Press the blackberries into the jelly, distributing them evenly. Continue to chill for 2 to 4 hours, until well set.

ELDERFLOWER AND BLACKBERRY JELLY SKEWERS

To make little bites for a party, double the amount of gelatin in this recipe to 6 full teaspoons. Pour into an 8- or 9-inch (20- or 23-cm) square baking dish. Set overnight in the refrigerator. Cut into 1-inch (2.5-cm) squares, or use a small cookie cutter to cut out 1-inch (2.5-cm) circles. Skewer one or two pieces on a toothpick or party pick with a whole fresh blackberry also skewered next to the jelly square. Chill until ready to serve, and pass a bowl of whipped cream for dipping.

HOLIDAY CRANBERRY GELATIN MOLD

Where would a chapter on fruit jellies be without at least one mention of the venerable holiday cranberry mold? Jellied cranberries are a staple of the Thanksgiving and Christmas meals, so why not go all out this year and do a pretty mold of cranberry jelly with real cranberries inside?

SERVES 8 OR MORE.
GLUTEN-FREE. DAIRY-FREE.

- 1 **(12-ounce / 340-g) bag fresh cranberries**
- ¾ **cup (180 ml) ruby port**
- ½ **cup (120 ml) pulp-free orange juice**
- ½ **cup (100 g) sugar**
- 1 **(3-inch / 7.5-cm) cinnamon stick**
- 3 **cups (720 ml) 100% juice cranberry juice blend, divided**
- 4 **tablespoons powdered gelatin**

Prepare a mold, glass bowl, or loaf pan that holds 6 cups (1.4 L) or more by spraying it lightly with baking spray or wiping it with neutral-flavor vegetable oil. Wipe out the bowl again with a paper towel, leaving only a faint residue of the oil behind.

Combine the cranberries, port, orange juice, sugar, cinnamon stick, and ½ cup (120 ml) water in a large saucepan. Simmer for 10 minutes, or until the berries have burst and the color has darkened slightly.

Pour 1 cup (240 ml) of the cranberry juice into a small saucepan and sprinkle the gelatin over the surface. Let it soften for 5 minutes, then warm the mixture over medium-low heat, stirring frequently, until the gelatin has completely dissolved. Whisk this mixture into the cranberries and stir in the remaining 2 cups (480 ml) cranberry juice. Pour into the prepared mold and cover loosely with plastic wrap. Chill for at least 12 hours.

When you're ready to unmold, loosen the edges of the gelatin with the point of a knife and dip the mold in a large bowl of warm water for about 2 minutes. Carefully flip it over onto a decorative plate. Serve chilled.

PEACH JELLY WITH CHERRIES

My husband grew up on a retired peach orchard, purchased by his parents so they could "move back to the land," farm, and build their own home away from the city. It was an idyllic place for a toddler, especially since there were still peaches everywhere. Despite eating peaches at nearly every meal as a baby, my husband craves them even now—so this fragrant summer jelly is for him.

MAKES 3 CUPS (720 ML) OR SIX SERVINGS. GLUTEN-FREE. DAIRY-FREE.

- 1 generous cup peach slices (from about ½ pound / 225 g fresh peaches), or 1 (15-ounce / 425-g) can peaches
- 1 cup (155 g) fresh cherries, pitted and halved
- 1 lemon, juiced (about 3 tablespoons)
- 6 teaspoons powdered gelatin
- 2½ cups (600 ml) peach juice or nectar

Arrange the peach slices, pit side up, in a spiral in the bottom of six small molds or a 1-quart (1-L) bowl or jelly mold. Spread the cherries over the peaches.

Mix the lemon juice and ½ cup (120 ml) water in a small saucepan. Sprinkle the gelatin over the surface and let it soften for 5 minutes. Warm the pan over medium-low heat, stirring frequently, until the gelatin is fully dissolved. Whisk in the peach nectar.

Slowly and carefully pour the mixture over the peaches and cherries, trying not to dislodge any slices. (If anything shifts, use a skewer or fork to gently nudge it back into place.) Chill for 4 hours or overnight. When ready to unmold, loosen the edges of the gelatin with the point of a knife and dip the mold in a large bowl of warm water for about 2 minutes. Flip it over carefully onto a plate. Serve chilled.

JELLIED ORANGE SLICES

This may be the most fun recipe in the entire book! Instead of pouring the jelly into cups or bowls, you pour it *back* into the orange-half shells and let them set. Then slice, just as if you're cutting a regular orange fruit. Everyone will be stumped—how did the jelly get inside the orange peel? It's fun to serve these on a plate with regular orange slices and watch people do a double-take!

**MAKES 24 TO 30 SLICES.
GLUTEN-FREE. DAIRY-FREE.**

- **6 tangerines, navel oranges, or blood oranges**
- **2½ teaspoons powdered gelatin**

Cut the oranges in half horizontally and juice them using a reamer—be careful not to split the skin. Gently scrape out the orange skins, removing any pith and strings and leaving behind as smooth a shell as possible. Place each orange shell in the well of a muffin tin.

Sprinkle the gelatin over ¼ cup (60 ml) cold water in a small saucepan and let it soften for 5 minutes. Strain the orange juice and measure it—you should have at least 1 cup (240 ml). Pour the juice into the pan with the gelatin and warm the mixture over low heat, stirring until the gelatin is completely dissolved.

Divide the mixture evenly among the empty orange skins. Chill for 4 hours, or until completely set. Trim away any excess orange peel above the surface of the orange jelly, and cut each orange half into wedges. Chill until serving.

PAPAYA FILLED
WITH COCONUT CREAM AND MANGO

This is a true fruit dessert—the papaya and mango get all the attention here! It's a simple dessert, too: Hollow out the seeds in the center of a papaya, and fill it with jellied coconut milk and some mango slices. Chill, then slice. It's a showstopper of color and fresh, ripe fruit. This is also very good when garnished with Toasted Coconut (page 50).

SERVES 6. GLUTEN-FREE.
DAIRY-FREE.

- 1 **(13.5-ounce / 400-ml) can coconut milk**
- 2½ **teaspoons powdered gelatin**
- 2 **tablespoons sugar**
- 1 **large papaya, 10 to 12 inches (25 to 30.5 cm) long**
- 1 **very ripe mango**
- ½ **lemon**

  Cinnamon, to serve

Shake the coconut milk can vigorously to stir up the milk and cream. Pour it into a small saucepan and whisk thoroughly. Sprinkle the gelatin over the surface of the coconut milk and let it sit for 5 minutes to soften. Warm the mixture over medium heat and whisk in the sugar for several minutes, until the gelatin and sugar have both dissolved. Turn off the heat and set the pan aside.

Slice the papaya in half lengthwise and remove the seeds. Hollow out the fruit just enough to provide room in both halves for about 1 cup (240 ml) liquid. Place the halves in a baking pan and stabilize them with crumpled aluminum foil so that they are level. Pour in the coconut mixture, dividing it evenly between the two halves.

Peel the mango and cut it into small cubes. Divide these between the two papaya halves, dropping them into the coconut milk mixture. Squeeze the lemon lightly over both halves, sprinkling them with juice. Chill for 2 hours, or until completely set. Slice crosswise into 1-inch (2.5-cm) slices and serve lightly dusted with cinnamon.

CHAMPAGNE JELLY
WITH RASPBERRIES

What's better than a glass of Champagne with a raspberry popped in? Nothing comes to mind, honestly. But if you're inclined to make a dessert out of it, this pretty Champagne or sparkling wine jelly is just the thing. Look for a dry sparkling wine—not real Champagne, actually, as it is quite expensive. I recommend a French Crémant or a Prosecco from Italy. Look for the "Brut" designation, which means it isn't too sweet.

MAKES SIX ½-CUP (120-ML) SERVINGS. GLUTEN-FREE. DAIRY-FREE.

- 1   **bottle (750 ml) dry sparkling wine, divided**
- 3   **teaspoons powdered gelatin**
- 2   **tablespoons sugar, or more to taste**
- 1½   **cups (185 g) fresh raspberries**

Pour 1 cup (240 ml) of the sparkling wine into a medium saucepan and sprinkle the gelatin over the surface to soften for 5 minutes. Warm the pan over medium heat and stir in the sugar. Continue to warm just until the gelatin and sugar are dissolved completely. Turn off the heat, pour in the rest of the sparkling wine, and whisk to combine.

Pour half of this mixture into a shallow bowl and put it in the freezer to chill quickly. Remove it after 15 minutes and whisk vigorously. Put it back in the freezer for another 15 minutes. (At no time should you leave the gelatin in the freezer for longer than 15 minutes.) Remove and whisk the mixture once more, then divide the now-viscous, partially set jelly among six Champagne flutes or wine-glasses. Divide the raspberries among the glasses, tumbling them together with the partially set gelatin. Divide the remaining gelatin mixture among the glasses. Chill for 2 hours, or until completely set.

EASY FLAVOR VARIATION
muscat or rosé jelly

You can make this with other sorts of wine as well. I particularly like it with a sweet Muscat and with sweeter pink rosé-style sparkling wines. Taste and adjust the sugar depending on the sweetness of the wine.

BASIC MILK JELLY

Milk jelly is a little different from panna cotta in that it has no cream and is both lighter and firmer. It's mainly used here for layering with other jellies—to provide a pretty contrast in both taste and texture. It sets opaque, too, so you get the contrast of glistening translucent fruit jelly with creamy white milk. Like panna cotta, milk jelly can also be infused with flavors, like spices and tea.

MAKES 2 CUPS (480 ML) OR FOUR SERVINGS. GLUTEN-FREE.

- **3 teaspoons powdered gelatin**
- **2 tablespoons sugar**
- **2 cups (480 ml) whole milk**
- **¼ teaspoon pure vanilla extract**

Pour ¼ cup (60 ml) water into a small saucepan and sprinkle the gelatin over its surface. Soften the gelatin for 5 minutes, then warm the pan over medium heat, stirring frequently, until the gelatin is fully dissolved. Stir in the sugar and continue warming until it is fully dissolved. Whisk in the milk and vanilla; pour into cups and chill or use as directed in a layered jelly.

EASY FLAVOR VARIATIONS
yogurt milk jelly

Substitute yogurt (I prefer full-fat, but low-fat and no-fat will work fine too) for 1 cup (240 ml) of the milk.

cinnamon milk jelly

Add ¼ teaspoon cinnamon to the mixture, or warm the milk and steep a cinnamon stick in it for 15 minutes before adding the milk to the gelatin.

lemon milk jelly

Add the zest of ½ lemon to the milk jelly just before chilling.

chocolate jelly

Stir 2 ounces (55 g) finely chopped chocolate into the warm milk jelly, until the chocolate is fully melted and incorporated.

nutella jelly

Replace ½ cup (120 ml) of the milk with an equal amount of Nutella and whisk vigorously to incorporate.

BEACH-GLASS JELLY SQUARES

Stained glass, marbled jelly, broken-glass Jell-O—this dessert has had many names, but the most familiar version is the stained-glass recipe from Jell-O itself. The idea is simple: Make a few flavors of Jell-O, let them set overnight, then cut them up into squares and tumble them together in a setting of sweetened condensed milk jelly. It's a sugar bomb and, to be honest, looks better than it tastes. But I love the concept, and I like it much better when executed by Bompas & Parr, those British jelly wonderboys. They mix real fruit jellies and bind them together with a lighter milk blancmange.

My version is closer to theirs, using white grape, cherry, and lime jellies for a lighter and more natural jelly square, and yogurt milk jelly—more interesting and tangy than a plain milk blancmange. The colors are paler than those in the official Jell-O version, so I call these *beach glass*—softly colored with pale yellow, white, and pink.

MAKES ABOUT 24 SQUARES. GLUTEN-FREE.

- ½ batch Firm Fruit Jelly (page 140), made with cherry juice
- ½ batch Firm Fruit Jelly (page 140), made with white grape juice
- ½ batch Lemonade Jelly (page 144; prepared without the basil), made with lime juice and doubled gelatin
- 2 batches Yogurt Milk Jelly (page 155)

Make each of the fruit jellies and chill them for 4 hours or overnight. Remove them from the pans and chop them into rough squares or uneven chunks. Spread in a 9-by-13-inch (23-by-33-cm) ungreased baking dish.

Make the yogurt milk jelly and cool the mixture for at least 15 minutes, so it is no longer warm, but not yet set. Pour it evenly over the chopped jelly in the baking dish and refrigerate for at least 4 hours, until completely set. Cut the jelly into squares and serve it out of the pan or on a serving plate.

COFFEE AND CREAM JELLY CUPS

Here's a delicious dessert for lovers of coffee (and cream). It has dark coffee, with just a hint of cream to give it some weight and richness, and a creamy top spiked with espresso powder. Use your favorite dark-roast coffee for this—for maximum flavor, I recommend brewing in a French press, although drip coffee is fine as well.

MAKES ¾-CUP (180-ML) SERVINGS. GLUTEN-FREE.

- **2 teaspoons powdered gelatin**
- **3 tablespoons sugar**
- **2½ cups (600 ml) strong, freshly brewed coffee, cooled**
- **¼ cup (60 ml) cream, at room temperature**
- **2 tablespoons brandy (optional)**
- **½ batch Vanilla Panna Cotta (page 104)**
- **½ teaspoon espresso powder (not ground espresso beans; see Sources, page 213)**
- **Whipped cream (see page 167), to serve**
- **Chocolate powder, to serve (optional)**

Sprinkle the gelatin over ¼ cup (60 ml) water in a small saucepan. Let it soften for 5 minutes, then warm the pan over low heat, stirring frequently, until the gelatin is completely dissolved. Stir in the sugar until it is completely dissolved as well.

Pour the mixture into a bowl and whisk it with the brewed coffee and cream. Add the brandy, if using. Divide it among six small cups and chill until just set, about 1 hour.

Meanwhile, prepare the panna cotta as directed and stir in the espresso powder. Let this cool at room temperature until it is barely warm. When the coffee jelly is just set, divide the panna cotta mixture evenly among the cups. Return the cups to the fridge and chill for 2 hours, or until set.

Serve with a dollop of whipped cream and chocolate powder, if desired.

PEACH JELLY TERRINE WITH YOGURT

This is a truly gorgeous terrine—peach jelly with real peaches suspended inside, layered with creamy yogurt jelly in the center.

MAKES 6 TO 8 SLICES. GLUTEN-FREE.

2 **cups very ripe and fragrant sliced and peeled peaches (from about 1 pound / 455 g peaches), or 2 (15-ounce / 425-g) cans peaches**

2 **cups (480 ml) peach juice, divided**

4½ **teaspoons powdered gelatin**

1 **lemon, juiced (about 3 tablespoons), divided**

1 **batch Yogurt Milk Jelly (page 155)**

¼ **teaspoon nutmeg**

Mint sprigs, to garnish

Lightly grease a 6-cup (1.4-L) loaf pan with a neutral-flavor vegetable oil, then wipe out the excess with a clean paper towel. Arrange half of the peach slices in the pan and put the pan in the freezer for 15 minutes to begin chilling.

Pour ½ cup (120 ml) of the peach juice into a small saucepan and sprinkle the gelatin evenly over the surface. Let the gelatin soften for 5 minutes. Warm the pan over medium-low heat, stirring frequently, until the gelatin is fully dissolved. Remove the pan from the heat and whisk in the remaining peach juice and 2 tablespoons of the lemon juice.

Pour 1 cup (240 ml) of the peach juice mixture into the prepared loaf pan. Put it in the freezer for 15 minutes to chill quickly (don't leave it there longer than 15 minutes, as true freezing destroys gelatin's thickening power). Transfer the pan to the fridge.

Meanwhile, make the yogurt milk jelly and stir the remaining 1 tablespoon lemon juice and the nutmeg into it. After about 30 minutes, when the peach gelatin is firm enough to not stick to your finger when pressed, pour the entire amount of cooled milk jelly over it, using a back-and-forth motion. Return the pan to the fridge to chill.

When the milk jelly has chilled completely, add the second layer of peaches and pour the remaining peach jelly mixture over them.

Cover and chill the terrine overnight. When you're ready to unmold it, dip the pan up to the brim in a bowl of warm water for 2 minutes. Loosen the edges of the jelly with the point of a knife, then turn it over quickly onto a rectangular platter. Serve in slices, garnished with mint.

SPICED APPLE CIDER AND CINNAMON CREAM TERRINE

Most of these jelly desserts are intended for the summertime, when cold jelly slurped off a spoon sounds most refreshing. But here's one that is perhaps best suited to autumn, with layers of cinnamon-spiked milk jelly and apple cider layered together like hot cider with a whipped cream topping.

MAKES 6 TO 8 SLICES.
GLUTEN-FREE.

3 cups (720 ml) unfiltered apple cider, divided

1/4 cup (50 g) sugar

1 (3-inch / 7.5-cm) cinnamon stick

2 pods star anise

2 1/2 tablespoons powdered gelatin

1 batch Cinnamon Milk Jelly (page 155)

Lightly grease a 6-cup (1.4-L) loaf pan with a neutral-flavor vegetable oil, then wipe out the excess with a clean paper towel. Put the pan in the freezer to begin chilling.

In a saucepan, stir together 2 1/2 cups (600 ml) of the apple cider, the sugar, cinnamon stick, and star anise and bring to a boil over medium-high heat. Cover and reduce the heat to low. Simmer for 20 minutes, or until the cider is very fragrant and spicy. Let the mixture cool for 1 hour, then strain to remove the spices.

Pour the remaining 1/2 cup (120 ml) cider into a small saucepan, sprinkle the gelatin evenly over the surface, and let it soften for 5 minutes. Warm the pan over medium heat, stirring frequently, until the gelatin is fully dissolved. Whisk the mixture into the spiced cider.

Pour 1 cup (240 ml) of the cider mixture into the prepared loaf pan. Put it in the freezer for 15 minutes to chill quickly (don't leave it there longer than 15 minutes, as true freezing destroys gelatin's thickening power). Transfer the pan to the fridge.

Meanwhile, make the cinnamon milk jelly as directed and set it aside to cool for about 15 minutes. When the first layer of cider jelly is still a little sticky but releases your finger when pressed (after about 30 minutes in the fridge), pour half the milk jelly over it, using a back-and-forth motion. Return the pan to the fridge.

Repeat as the layers chill, adding a second layer of cider jelly, and a second layer of milk jelly. Finish with a final layer of cider jelly.

Cover and chill the terrine overnight. When you're ready to unmold it, dip the pan up to the brim in a bowl of warm water for 2 minutes. Loosen the edges of the jelly with the point of a knife, then turn it over quickly onto a rectangular platter. Serve in slices.

ROOT BEER AND CREAM SODA TERRINE

Root beer and cream soda—a classic combo! This fun jelly is a *terrine*—a layered dessert molded in a loaf pan and cut into slices. The original terrines were not necessarily loaf-shaped, and they definitely weren't sweet—they were savory molds of meat scraps cooked together into soft pâtés and spreads. But the word has come to signify anything molded in a loaf pan, so I freely grab it here.

**MAKES 6 TO 8 SLICES.
GLUTEN-FREE.**

3½ **cups (840 ml) root beer, divided**

4 **teaspoons powdered gelatin**

1 **batch Basic Milk Jelly
(page 155)**

2 **teaspoons pure vanilla extract**

Lightly grease a 4-cup (1-L) loaf pan with a neutral-flavor vegetable oil, then wipe out the excess with a clean paper towel. Put the pan in the freezer to chill for about 15 minutes.

Pour 3 cups (720 ml) of the root beer into a small saucepan and bring it to a boil over high heat. Lower the heat to medium and boil for 20 minutes, stirring occasionally, until the root beer is reduced by half. Turn off the heat.

Pour the remaining ½ cup (120 ml) root beer into a small saucepan and sprinkle the gelatin evenly over the surface. Let the gelatin soften for 5 minutes. Warm the pan over medium heat, stirring frequently until the gelatin is fully dissolved. Remove the pan from the heat and whisk in the reduced root beer.

Pour half of the root beer mixture into the chilled loaf pan. Return the pan to the freezer for 15 minutes to chill quickly (don't leave it there longer than 15 minutes, as true freezing destroys gelatin's thickening power). Transfer the pan to the fridge.

Meanwhile, make the milk jelly as directed, stirring in the additional 2 teaspoons vanilla along with the vanilla already called for in the recipe. Set aside to cool.

After about 30 minutes, when the root beer gelatin is sticky but releases your finger when pressed, layer half the milk jelly onto it, using a back-and-forth motion. Return the pan to the fridge to chill.

Repeat as the layers chill—adding a second layer of root beer jelly, and a second layer of milk jelly.

Cover and chill overnight. When you're ready to unmold the terrine, dip the pan up to the brim in a bowl of warm water for 2 minutes. Loosen the edges of the jelly with the point of a knife, then turn it over quickly onto a rectangular platter. Serve in slices.

6
WHIPPED CREAM DESSERTS & FLUFFS

Whipped cream can be a dessert all on its own. Add a little sugar and fresh strawberries—this is heaven on earth. In this chapter, we take a look at whipped cream and a few of the easy, classic desserts that put it front and center. For example, there's the fruit fool—a simple dessert that consists of two things: cooked fruit or curd folded together with whipped cream. You can find recipes that are more complex and tarted up with gelatin or chocolate, but why mess with a good thing? You can even skip fresh fruit—just warm some jam and fold that through the whipped cream instead. I prefer it with a swirl of homemade fruit compote, though, and rhubarb is perhaps the most traditional.

And then there's fluff—fluff! I just feel that the word, used in this context, should always have an exclamation point after it, don't you? It sounds so charming—promising something light and, yes, fluffy. What is a fluff? It's a very old-fashioned sort of dessert, made with whipped jelly folded together with whipped cream.

HOW TO MAKE WHIPPED CREAM
(CRÈME CHANTILLY)

Whipped cream is a welcome companion to almost any sort of pudding. A dollop of cream lightens each bite of a rich budino, and it makes a mild vanilla pudding that much more luxurious. Here are some tips and instructions for making whipped cream.

Crème chantilly is a fancy name for simple sweetened whipped cream. If your whipped cream has a little sugar added, get swanky and introduce your dessert as *Chocolate Pudding with Crème Chantilly*!

Whatever you choose to call it, when we talk about whipped cream, this is what we mean: soft peaks of real cream, lightly sweetened and flavored with vanilla.

MAKES ABOUT 2 CUPS (480 ML). GLUTEN-FREE.

- 1 **cup (240 ml) cream**
- 1 **tablespoon powdered sugar, or to taste**
- 1 **teaspoon pure vanilla extract**
- **Pinch salt**

Pour the cream into the bowl of a stand mixer, or use a large wide bowl and a hand mixer. (You can also use a blender, food processor, or stick blender.) Add the sugar, vanilla, and salt, and beat on low—increasing to medium speed as the cream thickens—until it holds soft peaks and has doubled in volume. Chill the cream in a covered container until serving time.

Do not overbeat the cream, as you will turn it into butter! (On the other hand, if you *want* to make butter, this is where you start, but that's a whole other story.)

HOW TO STABILIZE WHIPPED CREAM

If you are making your whipped cream ahead of time and want to keep it fluffy and light, chill it. Whipped cream can be stored in the refrigerator for a few hours. Other ways to stabilize whipped cream include whipping it along with a small amount of softened cream cheese. You can also add a small amount of dissolved gelatin, but most of the time this is too much work for me!

OTHER WAYS TO FLAVOR WHIPPED CREAM

Whipped cream easily absorbs flavors, so if you want to spice it up a bit, try adding dashes of spices (cinnamon, nutmeg, ground ginger) or flavoring extracts like rosewater, orange blossom, or almond.

WHIPPED CREAM AND FRUIT AS DESSERT

Whipped cream may be the most important dessert topper (what is pumpkin pie without it?), and as such, it can never be underestimated. Whipped cream gilds nearly anything and turns even plain fruit into a dessert. Fan out slices of pear on a plate and top them with nutmeg-kissed whipped cream, or put out little bowls of strawberries with whipped cream on top. Other ideas for fruit and whipped cream: apricots, applesauce or cooked apples, mango, banana, kiwi, or blackberries and raspberries tumbled together in a Champagne glass.

WHIPPED MASCARPONE

Mascarpone, the rich, soft Italian cheese, makes a lovely addition to whipped cream. This is a thick cream, one that can just about stand on its own as a dessert, topped with berries or syrup.

MAKES ABOUT 3 CUPS (480 ML). GLUTEN-FREE.

- 1 cup (240 ml) mascarpone cheese, softened at room temperature for 1 hour
- 1 cup (240 ml) cream
- 2 tablespoons powdered sugar, or to taste
- 1 teaspoon pure vanilla extract

Whip the mascarpone in the bowl of a stand mixer (or in a large wide bowl, using a hand mixer) until it is soft and lightened. Add the cream, sugar, and vanilla and beat on low—increasing to medium speed as the cream thickens—until it holds soft peaks and has doubled in volume. Chill it in a covered container until serving time.

CHOCOLATE WHIPPED CREAM

Chocolate whipped cream is a delicious alternative to regular whipped cream—it makes a great topping for a bowl of vanilla pudding.

MAKES ABOUT 2 CUPS (480 ML). GLUTEN-FREE.

- 1 cup (480 ml) cream
- ¼ cup (25 g) powdered sugar
- ¼ cup (20 g) cocoa powder
- 1 teaspoon pure vanilla extract
  Pinch salt

Pour the cream into the bowl of a stand mixer, or use a large wide bowl and a hand mixer. (You can also use a blender, food processor, or stick blender.) Beat on low, then increase to medium speed as the cream thickens. Add the sugar, cocoa, vanilla, and salt, and beat until the cream holds soft peaks and has doubled in volume. Chill it in a covered container until serving time.

COCONUT WHIPPED TOPPING

Coconut milk is rich enough to whip up into a very satisfying and creamy topping. It tastes of coconut, of course, but this is really delicious when paired with the right desserts. It's wonderful with chocolate mousse!

MAKES ABOUT 1 CUP (240 ML).
GLUTEN-FREE. DAIRY-FREE.

1 **(13.5-ounce / 400-ml) can coconut milk, chilled overnight in the refrigerator**

2 **tablespoons sugar, or to taste**

1 **teaspoon pure vanilla extract**

Open the can of chilled coconut milk and scoop out the hard, waxy coconut fat on top, stopping when you reach the liquid coconut water beneath. (Save the remaining thinner coconut milk for use in smoothies or soups.) Put the firm coconut milk in the bowl of a stand mixer (or use a large bowl and a hand mixer) and whip on high speed for 3 to 5 minutes, until the mixture holds soft peaks and has doubled in volume. Mix in the sugar and vanilla. Cover and chill for up to 3 days.

NONDAIRY ALTERNATIVES TO WHIPPED CREAM
WHIPPED CREAM OR COOL WHIP?

What's better: whipped cream or "whipped topping"? The taste of Cool Whip is more familiar than whipped cream to many of us. But it's not cream at all—it's an oil-based product made with sugar and milk proteins (so it's not dairy-free). Cool Whip has a lighter mouthfeel than whipped cream, and it's lighter in fat and calories as well. But it contains several things that many people now try to avoid, like hydrogenated vegetable oil and high fructose corn syrup. Personally I have a bit of nostalgic affection for Cool Whip (or whipped topping, as the generics are known!). But I mostly avoid it these days in favor of real, natural whipped cream.

If I want to have a nondairy accompaniment to a dessert, I usually make whipped coconut topping or simply drizzle the dessert with a sweetened nondairy creamer.

SWEET WINE SYLLABUB

Syllabub is a dessert from the history books, but there's no reason to relegate it to musty medieval banquets. This is a treat of a dessert, with just a handful of ingredients and a delicious taste. It's very simple: sweet wine and sugar, mixed together with whipped cream. It "curdles" the cream just a little bit, leaving it juicy and boozy and creamy. It's wonderful served with fresh summer berries or cherries. I call for both dry sherry and a sweeter wine, but you can also make this with all sweet wine.

MAKES SIX ½-CUP (120-ML) SERVINGS. GLUTEN-FREE.

- ⅓ cup (75 ml) sweet white wine, such as Muscat, or sweet red wine, such as ruby port
- ¼ cup (60 ml) dry sherry
- ¼ cup (50 g) sugar
  Grated zest of 1 lemon
- 1½ cups (360 ml) cream
  Strawberries, blackberries, or raspberries, to serve

Whisk together the wine, sherry, sugar, and lemon zest. Pour the cream into the bowl of a stand mixer (or use a large wide bowl and a hand mixer). Beat on low—increasing to medium speed as the cream thickens—until it holds soft peaks and has doubled in volume. Gently fold in the wine mixture. Chill in a covered container until serving time.

Divide the syllabub among six glasses or dessert cups and top with the strawberries, raspberries, or blackberries.

STRAWBERRY-RHUBARB FOOL

Rhubarb is a classic fruit for a fool; its sweet-and-sour taste has herbal notes of the garden, and this makes a pleasant contrast to the sweet, rich whipped cream.

MAKES FOUR ¾-CUP (180-ML) SERVINGS. GLUTEN-FREE.

for the strawberry-rhubarb compote
- ½ pound (225 g) rhubarb stalks, cut into ¼-inch (6-mm) pieces
- 1 cup (125 g) hulled and chopped strawberries
- ⅓ cup (65 g) sugar
- 2 long strips lemon peel

for the whipped cream
- 1 cup (240 ml) cream
- 1 tablespoon powdered sugar
- 1 teaspoon pure vanilla extract

Combine the rhubarb, strawberries, sugar, and ¼ cup (60 ml) water in a saucepan with the lemon peel. Bring the mixture to a simmer and cook for 10 minutes, or until the rhubarb has just begun to soften. Transfer the compote to a bowl and refrigerate it for at least 1 hour, until it is quite cold.

Whip the cream with the sugar and vanilla until soft peaks form and the cream has doubled in volume. Fold about two-thirds of the compote into the cream. Divide the mixture among four glasses or dessert bowls and chill for 1 hour, or until serving time. Top each dish with the remaining compote before serving.

// STRAWBERRY-RHUBARB FOOL

LEMON AND CITRUS CURD

Lemon curd is pure, sweet lemon flavor solidified into a creamy spread. It's quite easy to make, and it's an elegant mix-in to a whipped cream dessert. Try a whipped cream fool with lemon curd and fresh strawberries folded into the cream. Heaven!

This is a simple—even foolproof—way to make lemon curd. It uses a method (which I learned from one of Ina Garten's recipes) of beating all the ingredients together before cooking. I especially like this made with the sweeter, thin-skinned Meyer lemons, which are in season and abundant during the winter—especially in California.

MAKES 2½ CUPS (600 ML). GLUTEN-FREE.

- ½ cup (115 g) unsalted butter, very soft
- 1 cup (200 g) sugar
- 3 to 4 large lemons, zested and juiced (about ½ cup / 120 ml juice)
- 5 large eggs

Cream the butter in the bowl of a stand mixer (or in a large bowl, using a hand mixer) until soft and whipped. Beat in the sugar and the lemon zest until light and fluffy. Add the eggs, one at a time. Whip in the lemon juice and continue to whip until it is incorporated (the mixture may look curdled at this point, which is normal).

Pour the curd into a saucepan and cook over medium-low heat, stirring frequently and whisking occasionally, for 10 minutes, or until the curd thickens and coats the back of a spoon. (If you have a candy thermometer and want to track the temperature, the curd will thicken at about 170°F / 77°C.) Don't let the mixture boil, as this will create lumps. If it does boil, however, you can strain the finished curd through a fine-mesh sieve.

Store in the refrigerator for up to 2 weeks.

EASY FLAVOR VARIATIONS
lime curd

For a lime curd, substitute lime juice for the lemon juice; you'll need 5 to 6 limes.

clementine or orange curd

For a zesty orange curd, substitute pulp-free orange juice for the lemon juice; you'll need about 3 large oranges or 6 to 8 clementines.

STRAWBERRY AND BERRY CURD

Lemon curd is perhaps the best-known curd, but citrus isn't the only fruit that makes a delicious spreadable curd. Try this strawberry version, or substitute an equal amount of raspberries. It will be softer than a citrus curd, more like a creamy sauce.

MAKES 3 CUPS (720 ML).
GLUTEN-FREE.

1½ cups (216 g) strawberries, hulled

1 cup (200 g) sugar, divided

1 lemon, juiced (about 3 tablespoons)

½ cup (115 g) unsalted butter, very soft

5 large egg yolks

Puree the strawberries with half of the sugar and ½ cup (120 ml) water in a blender or food processor and strain the mixture through a fine-mesh sieve into a bowl. Stir in the lemon juice, and measure out ½ cup (120 ml) of the juice and set it aside. (Reserve any remaining puree or juice for another use.)

Cream the butter in the bowl of a stand mixer (or in a large bowl, using a hand mixer) until it is soft and whipped. Beat in the remaining sugar until light and fluffy. Add the egg yolks, one at a time. Whip in the strawberry puree and continue whipping until the mixture is very smooth.

Pour this mixture into a saucepan and cook over medium heat, stirring nearly constantly, for 10 minutes, or until the curd thickens and coats the back of a spoon. (If you have a candy thermometer and want to track the temperature, the curd will thicken at about 170°F / 77°C.) Don't let the mixture boil, as this will create lumps.

Pour the thickened mixture through a fine-mesh strainer, if desired. Store in the refrigerator for up to 2 weeks.

COFFEE FLUFF
WITH CHOCOLATE FLAKES

This is the first fluff I ever fell in love with! It's dark and coffee-flavored, yet light and creamy.

MAKES ABOUT EIGHT ½-CUP (120-ML) SERVINGS. GLUTEN-FREE.

¼ cup (28 g) ground coffee

¼ cup (55 g) packed light brown sugar

5 teaspoons powdered gelatin

2 cups (480 ml) cream

3 tablespoons whisky, such as Jack Daniels (optional)

1 teaspoon pure vanilla extract

¼ teaspoon salt

Bittersweet chocolate bar, for shavings

Heat 2 cups (480 ml) water to boiling. Set aside to cool for 5 minutes, then pour it over the ground coffee and steep for 5 minutes. Strain (use a French press or very fine-mesh strainer) into a bowl. Whisk in the sugar and sprinkle the gelatin on top. Let the gelatin soften for 5 minutes, then whisk vigorously until it is thoroughly dissolved. Pour the mixture into a wide, shallow dish. Refrigerate until it is set, about 2 hours.

Pour the cream into the bowl of a stand mixer (or use a large bowl and a hand mixer). Whip until it holds soft peaks. Fold in the whisky, vanilla, and salt. Remove the cream to a separate bowl, and whip the coffee gelatin, which should be quite firm by this point, until it is frothy and creamy. It will look like a thick, dark mocha espresso drink, or creamy café au lait, speckled with darker flecks of coffee jelly.

Fold the coffee jelly into the cream. Spoon the mixture into individual cups or a mold and refrigerate for 1 hour, or until set. The texture will still be quite soft and creamy. Use a vegetable peeler to shave chocolate flakes off the bar to garnish.

THE ELEMENTS OF FLUFF

I first discovered fluff in one of the wonderful essays by Laurie Colwin, the late columnist for Gourmet. She wrote short, sweet, yet rather trenchant pieces about her expeditions in home cooking, exploring ingredients and her experiences with them. She gives general instructions for coffee fluff in her essay on coffee, and I tweaked it just a bit until I had something that suited my taste.

The basic method for fluff goes like this:

1 **Make a batch of fruit jelly:** Use any of the recipes in this book.

2 **Whip the fruit jelly:** After the jelly is firmly set, whip it into a frothy mass.

3 **Whip the cream:** Whip chilled cream until it holds soft peaks.

4 **Fold the jelly and cream together:** Fold the two together and refrigerate for a short time, just until they are set. Together, they have a creamy yet jellied consistency, very light, with nubs of fruit jelly in the cream. Totally luxurious, and completely different!

LEMON FLUFF

Citrus-tart, creamy, and whipped—this lemon fluff is amazingly refreshing and satisfying all at once.

MAKES ABOUT EIGHT
1/2-CUP (120-ML) SERVINGS.
GLUTEN-FREE.

- 1 **cup (240 ml) cream**
- 2 **tablespoons powdered sugar**
- 1 **batch Lemon-Basil Jelly Skewers, made without the basil (page 144), completely set**

Whip the cream until it holds soft peaks, whisking the sugar in at the end.

Whip the chilled and firm lemonade jelly until it is lightened and creamy. It will look like a thick, pale-yellow froth. Fold this frothed jelly and the cream together. Spoon the mixture into individual cups or a mold and refrigerate again until set, at least 1 hour. The texture will still be quite soft and creamy, like a refrigerator version of ice cream.

NUTELLA FLUFF

Oh, Nutella, you're so irresistible, with that smooth chocolate and hazelnut deliciousness! Here's one more Nutella recipe—whipped Nutella folded together with whipped cream.

MAKES ABOUT EIGHT
1/2-CUP (120-ML) SERVINGS.
GLUTEN-FREE.

- 1½ **cups (360 ml) cream**
- 2 **tablespoons powdered sugar**
- 1 **teaspoon pure vanilla extract**
  Generous pinch salt
- 1 **batch Nutella Jelly (page 155), completely set**

Whip the cream until it holds soft peaks. Mix in the sugar, vanilla, and salt.

Whip the chilled and firm Nutella jelly until it is lightened and creamy. It will look like a thick froth. Stir this frothed jelly and the cream together. Spoon the mixture into individual cups or a mold and refrigerate again until set, at least 1 hour. The texture will still be quite soft and creamy, like a refrigerator version of ice cream.

BLOOD ORANGE FLUFF
WITH CHOCOLATE SHAVINGS

I love the sweet fruitiness of blood oranges. It takes quite a lot of them to make this creamy fluff, but the pink color is gorgeous and totally worth it for a special occasion. Don't skimp on the chocolate shavings, either—use a good-quality bar.

MAKES ABOUT EIGHT
½-CUP (120-ML) SERVINGS.
GLUTEN-FREE.

- 5 teaspoons powdered gelatin
- 8 to 10 blood oranges, juiced (2 cups / 480 ml)
- ¼ cup (50 g) sugar
- Salt
- 1½ cups (360 ml) cream
- 2 tablespoons Cointreau (optional)
- 1 teaspoon pure vanilla extract
- Dark chocolate bar, for shavings

Put ¼ cup (60 ml) water in a wide, shallow bowl. Sprinkle the gelatin over the top, and set it aside for 5 minutes to soften. Pour the orange juice through a fine-mesh strainer into a small saucepan set over low heat. Whisk in the sugar and a pinch of salt. Add the gelatin in its water, and whisk vigorously. Warm the mixture over low heat until the gelatin is thoroughly dissolved. Pour the gelatin into a wide, shallow container, such as a 9-by-13-inch (23-by-33-cm) pan, and refrigerate until the gelatin is set, about 2 hours.

Pour the cream into the bowl of a stand mixer (or use a large bowl and a hand mixer); add the Cointreau (if using), the vanilla, and a pinch of salt. Whip the cream until it holds soft peaks. Transfer the whipped cream from the mixer bowl to another large bowl and set it aside; wipe the mixer bowl clean.

Add the gelatin, which should be quite firm by this point, to the mixer bowl and whip until it is lightened and creamy. It will look like a thick pink froth. Stir this jelly and the whipped cream together. Spoon it into individual cups or a mold and refrigerate again until set, at least 1 hour. The texture will still be quite soft and creamy, like a refrigerator version of ice cream.

To serve, run a vegetable peeler down the side of the chocolate bar, creating curls and shavings to be sprinkled on top for garnish.

7

ICEBOX CAKES, PIES, TRIFLES & COOKIES

Puddings are all very well and good, but sometimes you just want a slice of cake. Some of my all-time favorite cakes are still no-bake, though—creamy and soft and filled with custard cream between the layers. The cakes and desserts in this chapter are for the most part very rich, and they are excellent choices for serving a big crowd.

Many of these desserts call for puddings from earlier in this book. They're layered between firm, crisp crackers or cookies and then, in some refrigerator alchemy, everything softens together to become more than the sum of its parts.

Each of these first few icebox cakes is a simple dessert, made without too much fuss: just graham crackers, pudding, and a swirl of something special, like lemon curd or marshmallow creme. They are easily adaptable to other flavors and combinations—just look to the custards in the first chapter of this book for filling inspiration. Want a vanilla cake with chocolate icing? Use Rich Vanilla Pudding (page 32) for the filling and layer it between graham crackers, finishing off with the Triple Chocolate Cream Icebox Cake's (page 184) chocolate icing. Looking for something nutty and rich? Try a Nutella pudding cake with Nutella Pudding (page 60) and top the whole thing off with whipped cream and toasted hazelnuts. The possibilities are endless.

This chapter also contains pies, like an Oreo pie and a marshmallow pie with a cornflake crust. Still no baking: These crusts are quick and unbaked, yet still crispy and firm.

One of my favorite sorts of desserts for a crowd is a trifle. Despite its name, the classic British trifle is a very substantial dessert. It consists of cake (or brownies, or any other sort of baked good you would like to use) layered with pudding and topped with whipped cream. The famous banana puddin' of Southern church potlucks is really just a home-style trifle.

Finally, there are no-bake cookies. I grew up in a huge family of eight children, and cookies were always in high demand. The magic of no-bake cookies was one of the quickest, easiest ways my mom could whip up a batch. My favorite was the simplest: classic cocoa and peanut butter no-bake oatmeal cookies. A neighbor kid came over one day, and my mom fed him and my brother a batch of these with cold milk on the porch. He looked up at her, wide-eyed, and said, "I don't want any milk. I don't want to wash the taste of these out of my mouth!"

No-bake cookies are simple and not usually very elegant—they can't hold a candle to fancy sugar cookies or *springerle* for looks. But they make up a lot of ground in taste, as they tend to be fudgy, chewy, crispy—sometimes all at once. This collection is a handful of no-bake cookies and bars that can stand on their own, proudly, as dessert—dessert with a taste you don't want to leave your mouth.

Most of these cookies are quite sweet, by necessity. Without a session in the oven to give this kind of cookie a firm bite, no-bake cookies need sweet, sticky things like honey and marshmallows to hold them together. I've tried to balance out that sweetness with an extra pinch of salt, or even spicy pepper.

NO-BAKE DESSERT TIPS AND TROUBLESHOOTING

These desserts are among the most trouble-free you'll find. But here are a few tips for success:

» For best results, have all your components chilled before you begin, unless the recipe specifies otherwise.

» Chill for the recommended time in the recipe, and don't let the cake sit too long afterward. Many of these will get soggy after a few days in the fridge.

GLUTEN-FREE ICEBOX CAKES AND DESSERTS

Most of the desserts in this book are gluten-free, but the major exceptions come in this chapter of recipes, many of which call for graham crackers, chocolate cookies, and other gluten-full store-bought ingredients. But there is no reason why you cannot use gluten-free equivalents for these things, if you are up for a little experimentation.

SERVING IDEAS

When making and serving icebox cakes and pies, I find that using a springform or removable-bottom pan really contributes to an elegant end result. Try building a graham cracker icebox cake in a 9-by-13-inch (23-by-33-cm) removable-bottom pan, like the excellent ones from Magic Line (see Sources, page 213). Chill until very firm, then gently run a knife around the edge and lift out the cake.

LEMON CREAM ICEBOX CAKE

Tender layers of nutty graham cracker, holding up lemon-spiked cream with swirls of intensely tangy lemon curd—this cake's vibrant lemon flavor never fails to delight. "This tastes *just* like lemon!" is a common reaction.

SERVES 8 TO 10.

- ¼ cup (56 g) unsalted butter, very soft
- 3 cups (720 ml) cream
- ½ cup (50 g) powdered sugar
- ¼ teaspoon salt
- 2 large lemons, zested and juiced (about 2 tablespoons zest and ⅓ cup / 75 ml juice)
- 25 to 30 graham crackers, from about 4 sleeves
- 1 cup (240 ml) Lemon Curd (page 172), slightly warmed, divided

In the bowl of a stand mixer (or use a large bowl and a hand mixer), whip the butter until very soft. Gradually whip in the cream. When it has been smoothly combined with the butter, add the sugar, salt, and lemon zest. Whip until the cream forms firm peaks, then slowly beat in the lemon juice. Continue beating until completely combined. The cream should still hold soft peaks.

Smear a small spoonful of the lemon cream in the bottom of a 9-by-13-inch (23-by-33-cm) baking dish. Lay down a layer of graham crackers and spoon ¾ to 1 cup (180 to 240 ml) of the whipped cream over the top. Drizzle with ¼ cup (60 ml) of the lemon curd. Repeat three more times, finishing with a top layer of whipped cream. (You will have four layers of graham crackers, and four layers of whipped cream.) Drizzle the final ¼ cup (60 ml) lemon curd over the top of the cake in three straight lines, then draw a knife through these lines perpendicularly, creating a streaked checkerboard pattern.

Refrigerate the cake for at least 2 hours, until the crackers have softened to a cakelike texture (test this by inserting a thin knife along the side and bringing up a few crumbs). This can be made up to 24 hours ahead of time, but it is best consumed within a day or two, as it will get soggy if it sits too long.

HOW TO MAKE A FRUIT AND CREAM ICEBOX CAKE

The recipes in this section represent some of my own favorite takes on the classic American icebox cake. But I also want to show you how easy it is to improvise and create this kind of crowd-pleasing dessert with any fresh fruit you have in season.

The method: Whip 3¼ cups (780 ml) chilled cream with ⅓ cup (35 g) powdered sugar, 1 teaspoon vanilla, and a pinch of salt. Thinly slice about 2 pounds (910 g) fruit such as strawberries, peeled peaches, mangos, kiwi, or banana—you should end up with about 4 cups (960 ml) thinly sliced fruit. Take 4 sleeves of graham crackers (24 to 28 crackers) and layer them with the cream and fruit to make four layers of crackers, finished off with the last of the whipped cream. Lay any remaining fruit on top, and chill the cake for at least 2 and up to 24 hours. This will serve a crowd—eight at least, and up to twelve or more.

TRIPLE CHOCOLATE CREAM ICEBOX CAKE

This cake was made for my friends Jeanne and April, who both have a pure and simple love of chocolate. They'll never pass up a chocolate dessert, and this cake is their kind of chocolate fun: whipped cream mixed with cocoa and melted chocolate, then sandwiched between chocolate graham crackers. When it all melds together under a topping of old-fashioned chocolate frosting, it's dark, creamy, triple-chocolate heaven.

SERVES 8 TO 10.

- 2 cups (480 ml) cream, divided
- 3 ounces (85 g) bittersweet chocolate, finely chopped
- 1 (8-ounce / 225-g) package cream cheese, softened at room temperature for 1 hour
- 3 tablespoons cocoa powder
- 2/3 cup (70 g) powdered sugar
- 1 teaspoon pure vanilla extract
- 1/4 teaspoon kosher salt
- 25 to 30 chocolate graham crackers, from about 4 sleeves

for the chocolate frosting

- 1/4 cup (56 g) unsalted butter
- 3 tablespoons cocoa powder
- 1/4 cup (60 ml) milk
- 1 3/4 cups (175 g) powdered sugar
- 1/4 teaspoon kosher salt

Warm 1/2 cup (120 ml) of the cream in a small saucepan. When it bubbles slightly around the edges, add the chocolate and remove the pan from the heat. Stir the mixture to combine and put it in the fridge to cool while you prepare the whipped cream.

Beat the cream cheese in the bowl of a stand mixer (or in a large bowl, using a hand mixer) until it is very whipped and soft. Beat in the cocoa, sugar, vanilla, and salt. Gradually add the remaining 1 1/2 cups (360 ml) cream, beating until the mixture comes together smoothly. Gradually add the chocolate mixture, by now at least slightly chilled. Beat for several minutes on medium speed until the mixture holds soft peaks.

Smear a thin layer of the chocolate cream in the center of a 9-by-13-inch (23-by-33-cm) baking dish. Cover the bottom with a layer of graham crackers and spread 1 cup (240 ml) of the chocolate cream on top of the crackers. Repeat two times and top with a final layer of graham crackers. (There will be four full layers of crackers, and three of cream.) Put the cake in the refrigerator to begin chilling while you prepare the frosting.

Warm the butter with the cocoa powder in a small saucepan over medium heat until melted and bubbly. Whisk in the milk and cook for 2 to 3 minutes, until it is bubbling and thick. Turn off the heat and whisk in the sugar, about 1/2 cup (50 g) at a time. Whisk, blend, or beat until smooth and glossy. Whisk in the salt. Pour the frosting over the cake and spread it while it is still warm. Refrigerate the cake for at least 2 hours, until the crackers have softened to a cake-like texture (test this by inserting a thin knife along the side and bringing up a few crumbs). This can be made up to 24 hours ahead of time, but it is best consumed within a day or two, as it will get soggy if it sits too long.

THE (ALMOST) PERFECT TIRAMISU

My husband used to hold a monthly tiramisu club with college friends, looking for *the* perfect recipe. It proved to be an elusive object. Many came close, but what in the end is perfection? This version is perfect for my taste: I like it boozy, and I also choose to make a cooked zabaglione custard to avoid raw eggs, which not everyone is comfortable with. Some people might like the ladyfingers a little softer; others might object to the cocoa powder dusting. Some people strenuously insist on using a raw-egg custard and whipped egg whites instead of the zabaglione and whipped cream. To each his own. Just think of this as a good place to start in your own quest for tiramisu perfection.

SERVES 6 TO 8.

- 5 **large egg yolks**
- ½ **cup (100 g) sugar**
- ½ **cup (120 ml) sweet Marsala wine (or ruby port)**
- 2 **cups (480 ml) mascarpone cheese, softened at room temperature for 1 hour**
- 1 **teaspoon pure vanilla extract**
- ¼ **teaspoon salt**
- 2 **cups (480 ml) cream**
- 1 **cup (240 ml) brewed espresso or very strong brewed coffee, cooled to room temperature**
- 2 **tablespoons rum (optional)**
- 7 **to 8 ounces (200 to 225 g) crisp *savoiardi*-style ladyfingers**

  Cocoa powder

NOTE // Use the true, traditional Italian *savoiardi* ladyfinger biscuits, which are crisper and can absorb more liquid without getting soggy. Look for them in Italian sections of the grocery store, in specialty markets, and online.

In a 2-quart (2-L) bowl, whisk the egg yolks by hand or with a hand mixer for about 3 minutes, until they turn pale yellow and are quite thick. Add the sugar and the wine and whisk to combine. Pour the mixture into a saucepan over medium heat, and cook for 5 to 8 minutes, whisking frequently and vigorously, until the mixture thickens and just begins to boil. Remove it from the heat.

In a large bowl, beat the mascarpone with the vanilla and salt until well combined and fluffy. Pour in the egg yolk and Marsala sauce (this sauce is called zabaglione) and fold the mixture together.

In the bowl of a stand mixer (or in a large bowl, using a hand mixer), beat the cream until it holds stiff peaks. Gently fold the whipped cream into the mascarpone mixture.

To assemble the tiramisu, mix the coffee and rum, if using, in a shallow dish. Dip one side of each ladyfinger in the coffee for no longer than 1 second, and lay it soaked-side up in an 8-inch (20-cm) square glass dish. Cover the bottom of the dish with half of the coffee-soaked ladyfingers, and spread half of the cream mixture over them. Repeat, creating another layer of ladyfingers and spreading the remaining half of the cream on top. Dust with cocoa (tapped through a fine-mesh sieve) and cover the dish. Refrigerate for 4 to 8 hours, until the cookies are softened to your taste. This can be made up to 24 hours before serving, but no more, as I find the biscuits are too soggy after this to be enjoyable.

TIRAMISU: THE FANCIEST ICEBOX CAKE

Many people assume that tiramisu is an old Italian dessert, as classic as pasta and meatballs. But evidence points to it actually being quite a recent invention that was created at a restaurant in Italy and quickly became popular all over the world. And it is really no different from the other icebox cakes in this chapter: It is made simply of dry cookies or biscuits covered with sweet cream and left to soften in the fridge. It's a little fancier than graham crackers and whipped cream, I suppose, but at its heart, tiramisu is just a homey icebox cake.

GINGERSNAP AND CINNAMON ICEBOX CUPCAKES

If icebox cakes are so simple, why not make icebox cupcakes, too? Well, here you go: one of the easiest little treats imaginable. Let me tell you, people go *wild* for these. They have all the magic of an icebox cake—you take two ingredients, and something much more than the sum of its parts emerges after a spell in the refrigerator—but they're smaller, cuter, and even more irresistible.

I chose gingersnaps for this particular recipe, but the flavor options for icebox cupcakes are wide open. Try Nilla wafers layered with Chocolate Whipped Cream (page 168) or chocolate wafer cookies with Whipped Mascarpone (page 168). I am particularly fond of using the Maria cookies found in the Mexican section of the grocery store; they are barely sweet, and terrific layered with lemon pudding. You could even make your own wafer cookies, like crisp Earl Grey tea cookies, and layer them with lemon-flavored cream. Use your imagination!

One last tip: These look extra-adorable when packed into wide-mouth ½-pint or 250-ml jars. Screw on the caps and they are easy to transport to a party.

MAKES 12 CUPCAKES.

- 48 crisp gingersnaps
- 1⅓ cups (315 ml) cream
- 2 tablespoons powdered sugar
- 1 teaspoon pure vanilla extract
- 1 teaspoon cinnamon, plus more to garnish
- Pinch salt

Set out twelve paper or foil muffin-cup liners and place a gingersnap in the bottom of each one. In the bowl of a stand mixer (or in a large bowl, using a hand mixer), whip the cream with the sugar, vanilla, and cinnamon until the mixture holds medium peaks. Spread a spoonful of cream over each gingersnap, and top with a second cookie. Repeat until you have four gingersnaps and four layers of cream in each paper liner. Dust with cinnamon (tap it through a fine-mesh sieve) and refrigerate for at least 2 hours. The cookies will almost certainly have softened to a cakelike texture, but you can test one by inserting a knife in the center to make sure it goes in easily.

THE FAMOUS CHOCOLATE WAFER ICEBOX CAKE

The simplest icebox cake of all is also the most famous. Nabisco Famous Chocolate Wafers are thin, dark-chocolate wafer cookies sold in transparent packages, and for many years the box has offered a fabulous recipe on the back. Let me paraphrase: Spread sweet whipped cream over a layer of wafers. Repeat many times. Refrigerate until soft and cakey. Serve, to chirps of praise from your dinner guests.

This storied cake is so simple it can hardly be called a recipe, and I wanted you to know that while it is sold by the slice at New York City bakeries like Magnolia, it's a snap to make at home.

If you want to get fancy, create stacks of cookies and turn them sideways in a loaf pan so they can be unmolded and sliced like a loaf. Or get *really* fancy and put some chocolate curls on top.

S'MORES PUDDING CAKE

Who doesn't like s'mores? I'd like to meet that person. Well, actually, for a long time, *I* didn't like them. Then I realized that the thing I objected to was the texture; a poorly made s'more is hard to eat, with a crispy graham cracker, hard chocolate, and a rubbery marshmallow falling apart and getting your hands all sticky.

Then I discovered that the key to a great s'mores dessert is to meld those layers together so there is soft chocolate-graham-marshmallow goodness in every bite. That's what this pudding cake does: graham crackers layered with rich chocolate custard and smoky marshmallows. It's easy and so totally over the top—it's a picnic dessert extraordinaire!

SERVES 8 OR MORE.

- 1 batch Rich Chocolate Custard (page 36)
- 25 to 30 chocolate graham crackers, from about 4 sleeves
- 3 cups (162 g) mini marshmallows
- 1 (13-ounce / 368-g) jar marshmallow creme

Smear a thin layer of custard in the center of a 9-by-13-inch (23-by-33-cm) baking dish. Cover the bottom with a layer of graham crackers and spread a third of the custard on top of the crackers. Sprinkle a third of the marshmallows over the custard, and torch them lightly with a kitchen torch, until soft and browned. (You can also put them under an oven broiler for 45 seconds.) Repeat twice, ending with a layer of graham crackers. (There will be four full layers of crackers, and three of pudding.)

Warm the marshmallow creme in the microwave or in a saucepan. Pour it over the top of the cake and spread while it is still warm. Refrigerate the cake for at least 2 hours, until the crackers have softened to a cakelike texture (test this by inserting a thin knife along the side and bringing up a few crumbs). This cake can be made up to 24 hours ahead of time, but it is best consumed within a day or two, as it will get soggy if it sits too long.

When you're ready to serve, use a kitchen torch or the broiler to brown the top of the cake until it's tan and toasty.

PEANUT BUTTER AND CHOCOLATE BUCKEYE PIE

I live in Ohio, where the Ohio State Buckeyes command an almost unbelievable amount of adulation and attention during football season (well, year-round, really). The official mascot, the buckeye, is a poisonous nut that grows on a very handsome native tree, and it's celebrated in all sorts of "buckeye" desserts—all of which include no actual buckeyes, but lots of peanut butter and chocolate. This pie is my own homage to my alma mater.

If you cannot find plain chocolate wafers, you can also use Oreo cookies; just twist them apart and scrape off the filling first.

SERVES 6 OR MORE.

- 22 to 25 **chocolate wafers, crushed (about 1½ cups)**
- ¼ cup (56 g) **unsalted butter, melted**
- **Pinch salt**
- 1 cup (240 ml) **Dark Chocolate Ganache (page 58), divided**
- 4 ounces (115 g) **cream cheese, softened**
- ½ cup (120 ml) **marshmallow creme**
- ½ cup (120 ml) **smooth natural peanut butter, with no sugar added**
- 3 cups (720 ml) **Peanut Butter and Honey Pudding (page 59), completely chilled**

In a medium bowl, mix the chocolate wafers, butter, and salt until crumbly and sandy. Press this firmly into a 9-inch (23-cm) pie pan. Put the crust in the refrigerator to chill for 10 minutes while you prepare the chocolate coating.

The ganache needs to be quite warm and easy to pour—the consistency of cold maple syrup. So warm it gently in the microwave or over low heat on the stove. Pour ½ cup (120 ml) of the ganache evenly over the chilled pie crust, tilting the pan to spread it up the sides of the crust. Put the pan back in the fridge to continue chilling.

In the bowl of a stand mixer (or in a large bowl, using a hand mixer), whip the cream cheese until it is very light and fluffy. Beat in the marshmallow creme and peanut butter. Gently fold in the pudding. Spread this mixture in the pie crust and drizzle the remaining ½ cup (120 ml) ganache over the top. Refrigerate the pie for at least 4 hours, or overnight.

STRAWBERRY TART
WITH WHITE CHOCOLATE AND OAT CRUST

Here's a simple summer dessert: a creamy filling with strawberries and lemon, poured into a crisp oat crust held together with white chocolate. It's sweet and nutty, creamy and tangy—everything a summer dessert should be.

SERVES 6 OR MORE.

- 6 tablespoons (85 g) unsalted butter
- ½ cup (48 g) old-fashioned rolled oats, roughly chopped
- 4 ounces (115 g) white chocolate, finely chopped, plus more to shave for garnish
- 1 generous cup (120 to 140 g) graham cracker crumbs, from 8 to 10 whole graham crackers
- 2 lemons, zested and juiced (about 6 tablespoons / 90 ml juice)
- 2½ teaspoons powdered gelatin
- 1 (8-ounce / 225-g) package cream cheese, softened at room temperature for 1 hour
- 1 (14-ounce / 397-g) can sweetened condensed milk
- 1 pound (455 g) strawberries, hulled and roughly chopped, divided
- ½ cup (45 g) sliced almonds, lightly toasted

Melt the butter in a skillet over medium heat, then stir in the chopped oats and cook for 1 minute. Stir in the white chocolate and cook, stirring frequently, until it has melted. Pour the mixture over the graham cracker crumbs in a large bowl and stir until it has a wet, sandy consistency. Quickly press the warm mixture into a 9-inch (23-cm) pie pan and place in the refrigerator to begin chilling.

Put the lemon juice in a small saucepan and sprinkle the gelatin over the surface. Let the gelatin soften for 5 minutes, then warm the pan over medium heat until the gelatin is fully dissolved. Turn off the heat and set the pan aside.

In the bowl of a stand mixer fitted with the paddle attachment (or in a large bowl, using a hand mixer), whip the cream cheese until very light and fluffy. Add the condensed milk, lemon zest, and gelatin mixture and beat until well combined. Gently fold in half of the strawberries and spread this mixture into the chilled pie crust. Top with the toasted almonds. Chill for a full 2 hours, or until quite firm.

Serve slices topped with the remaining strawberries and shavings of white chocolate.

SCOTCH, MARSHMALLOW, AND PECAN PIE
WITH CORNFLAKE CRUST

This pie takes a basic marshmallow pie filling and spikes it with smoky Scotch whisky for a much more grown-up treat. It's still very sweet, with a crispy crust made of cornflakes and caramel sauce, but the marshmallow filling is saved from being over-the-top sweet by that delicious smokiness of good Scotch. It's best to use a blended Scotch, as the mellower flavor lends itself better to a recipe like this.

SERVES 6 OR MORE.

- 1½ cups crushed cornflakes, from about 3 cups (75 g) whole cornflakes
- 2 tablespoons brown sugar
- 6 tablespoons (85 g) unsalted butter
- ½ cup (120 ml) Honey Caramel Sauce (page 43), divided
- 8 ounces (225 g) mini marshmallows
- ½ cup (120 ml) milk
- 2 cups (480 ml) cream
- ¼ cup (60 ml) blended Scotch whisky, such as Famous Grouse
- ½ teaspoon salt
- ⅔ cup (70 g) toasted pecans, finely chopped, divided

Mix the crushed cornflakes with the brown sugar, butter, and half of the warmed honey caramel sauce. Quickly, while the mixture is still warm, press it into a 9-inch (23-cm) pie pan and place in the refrigerator to begin chilling.

Combine the marshmallows with the milk in a large pot over low heat, stirring constantly. When the mixture is completely melted, remove the pot from the heat and cool completely. This will take at least 30 minutes. (You can speed the process by scraping the mixture into a separate bowl and refrigerating. Stir every 10 minutes.)

In the bowl of a stand mixer (or in a large bowl, using a hand mixer), whip the cream until it holds stiff peaks. Scoop out ¾ cup (180 ml) of the whipped cream and reserve it for topping the pie. Fold the Scotch and salt into the remaining whipped cream, then gently fold in half of the pecans and all of the marshmallow mixture. Spread this in the chilled cornflake crust.

Swirl the reserved whipped cream on top, and sprinkle with the remaining pecans. Drizzle with the remaining honey caramel sauce. Refrigerate for at least 4 hours, or until quite firm. Cut with a hot, wet knife for clean slices.

OREO ICEBOX PIE

When I brought this pie to a family dinner, my brother eyed it, and me, suspiciously. "Is this a *real* Oreo pie?" he asked. "Or some artsy culinary thing?" My five younger brothers have become resigned to my taste in lighter, less-sweet desserts; Oreos just aren't usually on the menu. I confess that I thought about trying to put a new twist on the venerable Oreo icebox pie, but then I came to my senses and kept it simple, classic, and decadent, with a crust made of crushed Oreos and a filling of cream cheese, whipped cream, and crushed sandwich cookies. As I told my brother, this Oreo pie is for *real*.

SERVES 6 OR MORE.

- 40 Oreos or other chocolate sandwich cookies, divided (from one 15.5-ounce / 439-g package)
- 6 tablespoons (85 g) unsalted butter, melted
- 1½ teaspoons powdered gelatin
- 1 (8-ounce / 225-g) package cream cheese, softened at room temperature for 1 hour
- 1¼ cups (300 ml) cream, divided
- ¼ cup (25 g) powdered sugar
- 1 teaspoon pure vanilla extract
- ½ teaspoon salt
- ¼ cup (60 ml) Dark Chocolate Ganache (page 58)

Crush 30 of the cookies into fine crumbs in a food processor or by hand. Remove about a quarter of these crumbs and set them aside. Mix the remaining crumbs with the melted butter. Press the mixture firmly into a 9-inch (23-cm) pie pan and put it in the freezer to chill while you prepare the filling.

Sprinkle the gelatin over ¼ cup (60 ml) water in a small saucepan and set it aside to soften for 5 minutes.

In the bowl of a stand mixer (or in a large bowl, using a hand mixer), whip the cream cheese until it is very soft and fluffy. Add 1 cup (240 ml) of the cream, the sugar, vanilla, and salt, and continue beating until the mixture holds firm peaks.

Add the remaining ¼ cup (60 ml) cream to the saucepan with the gelatin and warm the pan gently over low heat, whisking constantly until the gelatin has fully dissolved. Add this mixture to the cream cheese mixture and beat for an additional 3 minutes.

Fold in the reserved crushed cookies and spread the filling in the prepared pie crust. Drizzle with the ganache and refrigerate for at least 2 hours, or until firm. Garnish with the remaining 10 cookies, split in half or crumbled on top.

NO-BAKE LEMON CHEESECAKE
WITH BLUEBERRY SAUCE

Cheesecake can be such a hassle—baking in a water bath, trying to keep the top from cracking. This version is much simpler—and lighter, too—with a delicate, creamy texture and the sweet freshness of lemon. It's very good with the blueberry sauce included here, but it's also delicious plain or served with fresh fruit.

SERVES 6 TO 8.

- 2 **cups (280 g) graham cracker crumbs, from about 20 graham crackers**
- 2 **tablespoons sugar**
- ½ **cup (115 g) unsalted butter, melted**
- 3 **teaspoons powdered gelatin**
- 2 **lemons, zested and juiced (about ¼ cup / 60 ml juice)**
- 2 **(8-ounce / 225-g) packages cream cheese, softened to room temperature**
- ⅔ **cup (70 g) powdered sugar**
- 1 **teaspoon pure vanilla extract**
- 2 **cups (480 ml) cream**

Lightly grease a 9-inch (23-cm) springform pan with butter or baking spray. Mix together the crumbs and sugar, and stir in the melted butter. Press a thick layer firmly into the bottom of the springform pan. Place in the refrigerator to chill while you make the filling.

Sprinkle the gelatin over the lemon juice in a small saucepan. Let it soften for 5 minutes. Warm the pan over medium heat, whisking frequently until the gelatin is fully dissolved; set the pan aside.

In the bowl of a stand mixer (or in a large bowl, using a hand mixer), whip the cream cheese with the lemon zest, sugar, and vanilla until light and creamy. Add the cream and whip until the mixture holds stiff peaks. Whip in the gelatin mixture. Spread the filling over the chilled crust and refrigerate for 2 to 3 hours, until set.

Serve with blueberry sauce (recipe follows) poured over the cake or over individual slices.

BLUEBERRY SAUCE

MAKES 2 CUPS (480 ML).

- 2 **cups (296 g) blueberries, fresh or thawed frozen**
- 2 **tablespoons sugar**
- 1 **lemon, zested and juiced (about 2 tablespoons juice)**
- 2 **teaspoons cornstarch**
- 1 **teaspoon pure vanilla extract**
  Pinch salt

Stir the blueberries, sugar, and lemon zest together in a 2-quart (2-L) saucepan and bring them to a simmer over medium-high heat. In a small bowl, whisk the cornstarch into the lemon juice until smooth, then stir the mixture into the blueberry sauce. Boil for a full minute, or until the berries begin to pop open. Remove from the heat and stir in the vanilla and salt. Chill.

THE ULTIMATE BANANA PUDDING PARFAIT

When I say "pudding," the first thing that people think of, apparently, is "banana pudding!"—the statement is accompanied by gleaming eyes. "Like my grandmother used to make!" The classic banana pudding they are thinking of isn't a plain pudding—it's actually a parfait dessert of vanilla pudding layered with bananas and Nabisco's Nilla Wafers. This pudding takes that concept and lifts it up just a bit, with real homemade banana pudding.

This recipe requires that you make two of the puddings from chapter 1: Rich Vanilla Pudding (page 32) and Banana Pudding Supreme (page 48). You'll only use half a batch of each, so you can either divide each recipe or have pudding left over for later. You can also choose to make just one flavor, but I love it with the mix.

SERVES 8.

- ½ batch **Banana Pudding Supreme** (page 48)
- ½ batch **Rich Vanilla Pudding** (page 32)
- 1 (12-ounce / 340-g) box **Nilla Wafers**
- 4 large ripe bananas, peeled and cut into 1/4-inch-thick (6-mm) coins
- ⅔ cup (165 ml) cream
- 2 tablespoons sugar
- 1 teaspoon pure vanilla extract
- ¼ teaspoon salt
  Nutmeg, to garnish

Make and chill the puddings. Reserve about 1 dozen wafers to top the parfait.

Choose a large trifle bowl or any bowl that holds at least 2 quarts (2 L); spread a spoonful each of banana and vanilla pudding on the bottom of the bowl and swirl them together. Line the bottom of the bowl with vanilla wafers. Spread half of the banana pudding over the wafers and arrange about a quarter of the banana slices on top. Place another layer of wafers on top, and cover with half of the vanilla pudding, then another layer of banana slices.

Repeat with two more layers of wafers and bananas, and finish with the remaining vanilla pudding. As you go, insert a few wafers pressed up against the side of the bowl. (You will have four layers of wafers and bananas, and two layers each of banana pudding and vanilla pudding. Reserve a handful of banana slices for garnish.)

Beat the cream with the sugar, vanilla, and salt until it holds soft peaks. Spread on top and garnish with the reserved vanilla wafers, reserved bananas, and a dusting of nutmeg.

Chill for at least 2 hours before serving, until the cookies are slightly softened (insert a knife into a cookie layer and if it meets no resistance, it's ready).

EASY FLAVOR VARIATIONS
meringue topping

Nancie McDermott says that she and many fellow Southerners wouldn't consider this a banana puddin' without a meringue topping, which was an economical way to use up the eggs. You have all these whites left over after making pudding with egg yolks, so it makes a lot of sense to put them to use in a marshmallowy baked meringue. But that kind of meringue does need to go in the oven, and we're not turning on our ovens for any of these recipes!

Here's another way: Instead of topping the pudding with whipped cream, gently warm about half a jar of marshmallow creme until it is easily spread. Swirl this over the top of the banana pudding and arrange the reserved banana slices on top. Sprinkle the banana slices lightly with sugar, then torch them and the marshmallow creme until browned and golden.

"Banana puddin'," says Nancie McDermott, "is a family reunion recipe. At these reunions and church picnics, everyone made fried chicken, deviled eggs, banana puddin'. They all just had to be there."

Nancie McDermott (nanciemcdermott.com) is a warm ambassador for Southern sweets, with two books covering a broad range of old-fashioned sweets from the South (*Southern Cakes* and *Southern Pies*). I talked to her about perhaps the most classic Southern dessert of them all: banana puddin'. Its very ubiquity made it part of the landscape of Southern desserts, she explained.

But what is a banana pudding, and where did it come from? "It must have origins in an English trifle," says Nancie. "Custard layered with good things. But the South evolved as a rural culinary culture—not an urban one. So trifles would have been an aristocratic sort of thing until the twentieth century, when fancier desserts became more common. And this fancy idea merged with boiled egg custard—a very Southern recipe, very Kentucky. Also, bananas became widely available early in the twentieth century; almost overnight, they were everywhere in recipes and cookbooks!"

Banana pudding became very popular among people who would never have known ladyfingers, tea cakes, or sherry in the afternoon; it was a homey dessert with its roots in old British sweets.

Nancie says she still makes banana puddin' with Nabisco Nilla Wafers, in spite of fancy recent updates. "I cringe at disdain for the original," she says. "Banana puddin' was a celebration dish. It was *special*," says Nancie. "It's also really pretty until you start serving it and then it's an unholy mess!"

STRAWBERRY ETON MESS

This traditional English dessert takes its name from the famous boys' school, where it remains a favorite dish of students and parents alike. It's the sort of thing even a schoolboy could whip up—whipped cream (or ice cream) folded together with store-bought meringues and fresh summer strawberries. It's pure in its simplicity, and perhaps one of the better ways to enjoy truly good strawberries. I like mine with just a bit of extra strawberry.

SERVES 6. GLUTEN-FREE.

- 2 **pounds (910 g) strawberries, hulled and halved**
- 1/3 **cup (65 g) granulated sugar**
- 1 1/2 **cups (120 ml) cream**
- 1/4 **cup (25 g) powdered sugar**
- 1 **teaspoon pure vanilla extract**
  Pinch salt
- 4 **ounces (115 g) store-bought vanilla meringues, roughly crushed**

Set aside about 1 cup (144 g) strawberries as garnish, then roughly chop the rest. Combine them with the granulated sugar in a large bowl and set aside.

In the bowl of a stand mixer (or in a large bowl, using a hand mixer), beat the cream with the powdered sugar, vanilla, and salt until it holds stiff peaks. Gently fold in the chopped strawberries and meringues.

Spoon the cream into tall glasses or dessert bowls and place the reserved strawberry halves on top. Serve immediately, or chill for up to 1 hour.

EASY FLAVOR VARIATION
chocolate-strawberry eton mess

You can also use chocolate meringues to add a chocolaty dimension to this dessert.

CHOCOLATE AND VANILLA TRIFLE WITH CARAMEL SAUCE

Most of the recipes in this chapter depend on at least one prepared, store-bought ingredient like crackers, ladyfingers, or cake. This one uses brownies or dense chocolate pound cake—either will do. In this case, although I do not provide a recipe, I do recommend making the chocolate component yourself. It's very easy to whip up a batch of brownies or pound cake, and it will taste so much better than something from a store bakery. This is also a good way to use up leftover cake scraps or brownies; just throw them in a freezer bag and when you have enough, make this insanely rich and decadent trifle.

SERVES 8 OR MORE.

About 8 cups (2 L) cubed chocolate pound cake, from two 9-inch (23-cm) cake layers, or cubed cakelike brownies

1 **batch Rich Vanilla Pudding (page 32), well chilled**

½ **cup (120 ml) Honey Caramel Sauce (page 43)**

⅔ **cup (165 ml) whipped cream**

1 **tablespoon powdered sugar**

1 **teaspoon pure vanilla extract**

Spread about a third of the cubed cake in the bottom of a large trifle bowl (or any deep 3- to 4-quart / 2.8- to 3.8-L bowl). Spread a third of the pudding on top and drizzle with a small amount of the caramel sauce. Repeat twice, finishing with the third layer of pudding.

In the bowl of a stand mixer (or in a large bowl, using a hand mixer), whip the cream with the sugar and vanilla until it holds soft peaks. Spread it over the top and drizzle with the remaining caramel sauce. Refrigerate the trifle for at least 2 hours, or up to 24, before serving.

SPICED RUM AND PUMPKIN TRIFLE

This is perhaps my favorite trifle, with a rich eggy pumpkin custard and pound cake dipped in rum.

SERVES 8 OR MORE.

About 8 cups (2 L) cubed pound cake, from a 12- to 16-ounce (340- to 455-g) store-bought cake

½ **cup (120 ml) dark rum**

1 **batch Pumpkin Spice Pudding (page 42), well chilled**

1½ **cups (360 ml) whipped cream**

1 **tablespoon powdered sugar**

1 **teaspoon pure vanilla extract**

Ground cinnamon, to garnish

Dip the cake cubes quickly in the rum. Spread a third of the cubes in the bottom of a large trifle bowl (or any deep 3- to 4-quart / 2.8- to 3.8-L bowl). Spread a third of the pudding over the cake. In the bowl of a stand mixer (or in a large bowl, using a hand mixer), whip the cream with any remaining rum, the sugar, and vanilla until it holds soft peaks. Spread a third of this mixture over the pudding. Repeat twice, finishing with the third layer of cream.

Dust the trifle with cinnamon and refrigerate for at least 2 hours, or up to 24, before serving.

BLUEBERRY ANGEL FOOD TRIFLE

This is such an easy summer dessert—and so pretty, too. If you're in a patriotic mood, or looking for a dessert for the Fourth of July, replace half the blueberries with strawberries for a red, white, and blue treat.

SERVES 8 OR MORE.

About 8 cups (2 L) cubed angel food cake, from a 12- to 16-ounce (340- to 455-g) store-bought cake

1 **batch Rich Vanilla Pudding (page 32), well chilled**

4 **cups (592 g) blueberries**

²⁄₃ **cup (165 ml) cream**

1 **tablespoon powdered sugar**

1 **teaspoon pure vanilla extract**

Spread about a third of the cake cubes in the bottom of a large trifle bowl (or any deep 3- to 4-quart / 2.8- to 3.8-L bowl). Spread about a third of the pudding over the cubes and top with a quarter of the blueberries. Repeat twice, finishing with the third layer of pudding.

In the bowl of a stand mixer (or in a large bowl, using a hand mixer), whip the cream with the sugar and vanilla until it holds soft peaks. Spread it over the top and garnish with the remaining blueberries. Refrigerate the trifle for at least 2 hours, or up to 24, before serving.

SPICY PEANUT AND TOASTED COCONUT COOKIES

These cookies were inspired by Jeni Britton Bauer's Bangkok peanut ice cream—a tantalizing blend of toasted coconut and peanut butter cream, finished with a sharp prickle of cayenne pepper. The sweet-and-spicy juxtaposition is addictive, sending you back for bite after bite. Lucky for me, Jeni is a hometown fixture, with shops located dangerously near my house, and I can have this splendid stuff whenever I want.

I've worked these flavors into a crispy, sticky, spicy cookie—with just a tingle of spice.

MAKES ABOUT 24 COOKIES.

- 1 cup (80g) shredded unsweetened coconut
- 3 cups (135 g) chow mein noodles
- ½ cup (120 ml) honey or light corn syrup
- ½ cup (110 g) packed brown sugar
- 1 cup (240 ml) natural unsweetened peanut butter, well stirred
- ½ teaspoon pure vanilla extract
- ½ teaspoon kosher salt
- ¼ teaspoon cayenne

Line a large baking sheet with wax paper.

Heat a skillet over medium heat and add the coconut. Toast the coconut, stirring frequently, until it is light brown and crispy. Pour it into a large bowl and stir in the chow mein noodles.

Combine the honey or corn syrup and the sugar in a small saucepan and bring the mixture to a boil over medium heat. Turn the heat to low and simmer for 1 minute, then turn off the heat and stir in the peanut butter until fully incorporated. The mixture should look glossy. Stir in the vanilla, salt, and cayenne. Immediately stir the mixture into the coconut and noodles. Drop by spoonfuls onto the baking sheet. Cool for 10 minutes, or until set. Store in an airtight container for up to 5 days.

NO-BAKE COOKIES!

When it comes to no-bake cookies, don't forget: *Any* cookie can be no-bake! "Without a doubt, my favorite no-bake dessert is chocolate chip cookie dough," admits my friend David Leite, publisher of the always witty and entertaining online food publication *Leite's Culinaria* (leitesculinaria.com). "It's a guilty pleasure that I indulge in all summer long. I crumble it over vanilla ice cream, stir it into chantilly cream, and eat it right from the mixing bowl. And I'll admit there are times we get through a batch without ever having baked one cookie."

STICKY CARROT-CAKE BALLS
(CARROT *HALWA*)

Halwa (or halvah) is a catchall name for a sweeping array of sweets from all over the world, from sesame candies to crumbly desserts made with semolina. This particular *halwa* is one of my favorites: a thick, sticky paste of cooked milk and sugar, with fresh orange carrots folded in. It's fudgy and sweet, with the bright flavor of carrot cake.

MAKES 24 TO 30 BALLS. GLUTEN-FREE.

- 2 **tablespoons (28 g) ghee or unsalted butter**
- ½ **cup (62 g) cashew pieces**
- ½ **cup (80 g) golden raisins**
- 1 **cup (240 ml) full-fat ricotta cheese, well stirred**
- 1 **(14-ounce / 397-g) can sweetened condensed milk**
- 1 **cup (240 ml) whole milk**
- ⅓ **cup (65 g) sugar**
- 1 **teaspoon cardamom powder**
- 1 **pound (455 g) carrots, roughly shredded (about 4 cups)**
- 2 **cups (240 g) finely chopped pistachios**

Heat the ghee or butter in a 4-quart (3.8-L) saucepan over medium-high heat. Add the cashews and sauté for 2 to 3 minutes, until lightly browned. Add the raisins and cook for another 30 seconds. Remove from the heat and transfer to a bowl.

Stir the ricotta, condensed milk, and whole milk together in the saucepan. Stir in the sugar and cardamom. Bring to a simmer over medium heat, then add the carrots. Cook, stirring occasionally, for 30 minutes, or until the milk has mostly evaporated and the mixture is very thick. Stir in the cashews and raisins. Continue cooking for another 15 minutes, or until the pudding pulls away from the sides of the pan.

Scrape the mixture out into a shallow pan and place it in the refrigerator until it can be handled. Roll the carrot *halwa* into balls and roll these in the chopped pistachios. Chill until firm.

Refrigerate, covered, for 5 days, or freeze for up to 3 months.

ORANGE-WALNUT TRUFFLE BITES

I made literally hundreds of these cookies for a friend's wedding, pressing crisp cookie crumbs into melt-in-your-mouth cookies, coated in bittersweet chocolate. They're unexpected and fresh.

MAKES ABOUT 24 COOKIES.

- 1 cup crushed vanilla wafer cookies (130 g), from about 2 cups whole cookies
- 1 cup (100 g) powdered sugar
- ½ cup (60 g) minced walnuts
- ¼ cup (35 g) candied ginger, minced as finely as possible
- ¼ cup (32 g) cornstarch
- Grated zest of 2 oranges
- ½ teaspoon salt
- ⅓ cup (75 g) unsalted butter, melted and cooled
- 12 ounces (340 g) bittersweet chocolate
- 2 ounces edible wax (optional, see Note)

In the bowl of a food processor or chopper, blend the cookie crumbs with the sugar, walnuts, ginger, cornstarch, orange zest, and salt. Slowly add the butter, blending until it comes together in one sticky mass. Roll it into bite-sized cookie balls and place these in a parchment-lined baking pan. Freeze or chill until solid—about 4 hours.

Melt the chocolate and wax (if using) in a double boiler over low heat. After the balls have completely chilled, dip each one in the chocolate, using a fork and shaking it as you take it out of the chocolate. Place them on wax paper or parchment to cool.

Store in a covered container in the refrigerator for up to 5 days, or freeze for up to 3 months.

NOTE // Edible wax is paraffin, which is often added to chocolate to give it a glossy finish and to help it remain solid at room temperature.

PEANUT BUTTER–PECAN OATMEAL COOKIES

I do believe that peanut butter cookies are among the most irresistible treats known to mankind. Chewy and nutty, these cookies are altogether quicker and easier than a batch of the baked variety, and they're guaranteed to be melt-in-your-mouth soft.

MAKES ABOUT 24 COOKIES. GLUTEN-FREE.

- 4 tablespoons (56 g) unsalted butter
- ⅔ cup (165 ml) honey or light corn syrup
- ⅔ cup (150 g) packed dark brown sugar
- ½ cup (120 ml) sweetened condensed milk
- 1 cup (240 ml) creamy natural unsweetened peanut butter, well stirred
- 1 teaspoon pure vanilla extract
- ½ teaspoon kosher salt
- 3 cups (288 g) old-fashioned rolled oats
- 1 cup (110 g) chopped pecans, lightly toasted

Line two large baking sheets with wax paper or baking parchment. Melt the butter in a 4-quart (3.8-L) saucepan and stir in the honey or corn syrup, sugar, and milk. Bring to a rolling boil and boil for 2 full minutes. Turn off the heat and stir in the peanut butter until it is fully dissolved. Stir in the vanilla and salt. Fold in the oats and pecans.

Quickly drop by spoonfuls onto the baking sheets and chill for at least 30 minutes, until quite firm. These can be stored at room temperature, but they get a little soft and sticky, so it is best to refrigerate them, especially in warmer months. They'll keep, in an airtight container, for up to 5 days.

// CHOCOLATE PEANUT-BUTTER PRETZEL BARS

CHOCOLATE PEANUT-BUTTER PRETZEL BARS

These bars are an unholy mix of everything good that goes into a no-bake cookie: peanut butter, marshmallows, salty pretzels, puffed wheat—and a bit of chocolate to sweeten the deal. Finish it all off with a sprinkle of smoked salt to give it the aroma of a campfire.

MAKES 12 TO 16 BARS.

- 1 cup (220 g) packed brown sugar
- 1 cup (240 ml) light corn syrup
- 2 cups (108 g) mini marshmallows
- 3/4 cup (180 ml) creamy natural unsweetened peanut butter, well stirred
- 1 teaspoon pure vanilla extract
- 1/2 teaspoon kosher salt
- 4 cups (180 g) thin pretzel sticks, roughly chopped
- 4 cups (48 g) unsweetened puffed wheat cereal
- 2 ounces (55 g) bittersweet chocolate, melted
- 1/2 teaspoon smoked salt (or additional kosher salt)

Lightly grease a 9-by-13-inch (23-by-33-cm) baking dish. Combine the sugar and corn syrup in a 4-quart (3.8-L) saucepan and bring the mixture to a boil over medium-high heat. Turn off the heat and stir in the marshmallows until about half of them are melted, then stir in the peanut butter until well combined. Add the vanilla and salt. Mix in the pretzels and puffed wheat. Pat firmly into the prepared baking dish. Drizzle the melted chocolate over them and sprinkle with smoked salt.

Chill for 1 hour, or until firm. Slice into small bars with a hot, wet knife. Store in an airtight container at room temperature for up to 3 days.

CINNAMON GRAHAM AND MARSHMALLOW CLUSTER BARS

These graham cracker bars are crunchy and chewy and fragrant with cinnamon. Make sure you don't crush the crackers into crumbs; use a big knife to chop them roughly into chunky pieces.

MAKES ABOUT 18 BARS.

- 25 to 30 cinnamon graham crackers, from about 4 sleeves
- 4 tablespoons (56 g) unsalted butter
- 8 cups (432 g) mini marshmallows
- 1 teaspoon cinnamon
- 1/2 teaspoon ground ginger
- 1/2 teaspoon salt
- 1/3 cup (80 g) cinnamon chips

Lightly grease a 9-by-13-inch (23-by-33-cm) baking dish with baking spray or butter. Roughly chop the graham crackers into pieces about 1/2 to 1 inch (12 mm to 2.5 cm) wide and put them in a large bowl.

Melt the butter in a 4-quart (3.8-L) saucepan. Add the marshmallows and cook over low heat until completely melted. Stir in the cinnamon, ginger, and salt. Pour the mixture over the graham cracker pieces and stir until completely mixed. Press into the prepared pan and immediately sprinkle the cinnamon chips over the top. Let sit for at least 15 minutes, until the chips have softened. Use a knife to spread them into a thin coating over the top. Let set for at least 30 minutes, until cool and firm. Cut into bars to serve. Store leftovers in an airtight container at room temperature for up to 5 days.

NO-BAKE TRIPLE CHOCOLATE BROWNIES

This is a quick, easy recipe for rich chocolate treats that are halfway between fudge bites and brownies. They have a pleasantly nutty flavor, with crisp bits of crushed cracker and chopped hazelnut mixed in—and you can put them together in just a few minutes.

MAKES ABOUT 16 SMALL BROWNIES.

- 1 generous cup (100 g) graham cracker crumbs, from 8 to 10 whole graham crackers
- ½ cup (58 g) finely chopped roasted hazelnuts
- ¼ cup (20 g) cocoa powder
- ½ teaspoon kosher salt
- ¾ cup (180 ml) sweetened condensed milk
- 4 ounces (115 g) bittersweet chocolate, melted

Line an 8-inch (20-cm) square baking dish with two crossed strips of parchment or wax paper, letting the long ends hang over the sides of the dish. Grease lightly with butter or baking spray.

In a large bowl, mix together the crackers, hazelnuts, cocoa, and salt. Pour in the milk. (If desired, you can set the can in a pan of warm water to make it easier to scrape out and stir in the milk.) Pour in the melted chocolate and stir firmly to thoroughly combine, then scrape the mixture into the prepared pan. Cover with a piece of plastic wrap and press firmly into the pan. Chill for at least 1 hour, until firm enough to cut.

Lift the parchment paper to remove the brownies from the pan. Cut the brownies into small squares. They will be fudgy but quite firm. Store leftover brownies in an airtight container in the fridge for up to 5 days.

NO-BAKE MEYER LEMON BARS
WITH GINGERSNAP CRUST

Here's another chance to put lemon curd to good use—this time in tangy lemon bars with a spicy gingersnap base.

MAKES 9 BARS.

- 2 **cups gingersnap crumbs (220 g), from 3 to 4 cups whole gingersnaps**
- 2 **tablespoons granulated sugar**
- 6 **tablespoons (85 g) unsalted butter, melted**
- 2 **lemons, zested and juiced (about 6 tablespoons / 90 ml juice)**
- 1 **teaspoon powdered gelatin**
- 1 **batch Lemon Curd (page 172), made with Meyer lemons**

  Powdered sugar

Combine the gingersnap crumbs and granulated sugar in a bowl, and pour in the butter and 1 tablespoon water. Stir until the mixture is soft and well mixed. Press very firmly into a lightly greased 8-inch (20-cm) square baking dish and freeze while the filling is prepared.

Pour the lemon juice and 2 tablespoons water into a small saucepan and sprinkle the gelatin over the surface. Soften the gelatin for 5 minutes, then warm the pan over medium-low heat and stir until it is completely dissolved. Whisk it into the lemon curd. Spread the filling over the crust and refrigerate for 2 hours, or until set. Dust generously with powdered sugar just before serving and garnish with the lemon zest.

Refrigerate, loosely covered, for up to 5 days.

SOURCES

INGREDIENTS

Amaranth Found at health food stores and organic groceries such as Whole Foods Market. Look in the bulk grains section. It can also be bought online at Amazon (amazon.com).

Candied Flowers Candied flowers for garnishing puddings can be found online at Market Hall Foods (markethallfoods.com).

Chocolate Cups Edible chocolate cordial or shooter cups for serving pudding can be found in some restaurant supply stores and online at Amazon (amazon.com).

Chocolate Wafer Cookies Nabisco's Famous Chocolate Wafers can be found in some grocery stores and online at Amazon (amazon.com).

ClearJel Instant ClearJel can be found at King Arthur Flour (kingarthurflour.com).

Elderflower Syrup IKEA carries their own brand of syrup (called SAFT FLÄDER) and it can be purchased in-store. Monin brand syrup can be purchased online at Amazon (amazon.com).

Espresso Powder This can be found in specialty cooking stores such as Williams-Sonoma and Sur La Table.

Fever-Tree Ginger Ale Available nationwide in grocery stores and specialty markets such as Cost Plus World Market.

Ladyfingers Traditional *savoiardi* ladyfinger cookies can be found in some specialty food stores such as Whole Foods Market and online at Amazon (amazon.com).

Malted Milk Powder Carnation and NOW Foods brands of malted milk powder are widely available in grocery stores and health food stores.

Maple Syrup, Grade B This darker, more robust style of maple syrup is widely available in grocery stores.

Marshmallow Creme Marshmallow Fluff is available in the baking aisle of most major grocery stores.

Orange Blossom Water This can be found in Middle Eastern and Indian grocery stores, and online at Amazon (amazon.com).

Q Ginger Q Ginger ginger ale is available in some Williams-Sonoma and Whole Foods Market locations, as well as online at Amazon (amazon.com).

Quinoa Look for golden quinoa in the rice section of the grocery store, or in the bulk bins at health food or organic groceries.

Rosewater This can be found in Middle Eastern and Indian grocery stores, and online at Amazon (amazon.com).

Semiya Noodles Semiya noodles can be found in Indian groceries. Vermicelli can be substituted.

Tapioca Pearls Whole tapioca pearls, such as those from Bob's Red Mill, can be found in grocery stores or online at Amazon (amazon.com).

Vanilla Beans Vanilla beans can be found in any grocery store, but I find it is best to buy whole beans online, in bulk for best prices. Two good places to check: Rodelle (rodellevanilla.elsstore.com) and the eBay-based Vanilla Products USA (stores.ebay.com/Vanilla-Products-USA).

Vanilla Extract It's important to use pure vanilla extract. I prefer Nielsen-Massey Mexican vanilla, but any pure extract will do. Look for it in grocery stores or online at King Arthur Flour (kingarthurflour.com).

Vegan Jel, Unflavored In my opinion, the best vegetarian substitute for gelatin. It can be found in limited supply at health food stores and organic groceries and online at Amazon (amazon.com).

White Chocolate It's important to use high-quality white chocolate in recipes that call for it. I recommend E. Guittard (available at Williams-Sonoma stores) and Green & Black's Organic White Chocolate with Vanilla, (available nationwide in grocery stores and online at Amazon (amazon.com).

DISHES AND TOOLS

Cups, Ramekins, and Spoons: I have a large number of little cups and ramekins. Look at flea markets, thrift stores, and junk shops for interesting ceramics and vintage china. Etsy (etsy.com) and eBay (eBay.com) are also good sources. The same goes for spoons; if you want a special set of pudding spoons, look in these places for vintage silver or flatware. Other favorite sources for interesting, pretty china and flatware: Leif (leifshop.com), Anthropologie (anthropologie.com), BHLDN (bhldn.com), and West Elm (westelm.com).

Jelly Molds: Vintage jelly molds add flair to shaped jellies and panna cotta. Look for vintage copper molds in antique stores and online at eBay (ebay.com) and Etsy (etsy.com), and for new ones at Amazon (amazon.com).

Kitchen Torches: Kitchen specialty shops such as Williams-Sonoma and Sur La Table sell small butane kitchen torches for about $20. You can also find them online at Amazon (amazon.com), or skip the butane torch altogether and just use a household propane torch from the hardware store.

Pudding Pop Molds: For pudding pops, I like the retro-shaped molds from Tovolo, which can be found at Amazon (amazon.com) and in kitchen and household supply stores.

Removable-Bottom Cake Pans: A removable-bottom cake pan (such as the Parrish Magic Line 9-by-13-inch pan) and a round springform pan are both helpful for cheesecake and no-bake cakes. Look for these at bakeware specialty stores and at Amazon (amazon.com).

Trifle Bowl: A big pretty trifle bowl is great for serving layered puddings and trifles. Look for these on sale at shops like T.J. Maxx and Cost Plus World Market. Crate & Barrel always carries them also.

BIBLIOGRAPHY

Here are some books I found illustrative, helpful, inspirational, and otherwise useful while writing this one. If you've enjoyed this book, I highly recommend that you pick up one or two of these as well. Special thanks to those people who agreed to be interviewed for this book; I end with a list of their own Web sites, so you can enjoy more of their expertise and writing.

REFERENCE AND PUDDING INSPIRATION

Belanger, Victoria. *Hello, Jell-O! 50+ Inventive Recipes for Gelatin Treats and Jiggly Sweets.* Ten Speed Press, 2012.

Bompas, Sam and Harry Parr. *Jellymongers: Glow-in-the-Dark Jelly, Titanic Jelly, Flaming Jelly.* Sterling Epicure, 2011.

Bullock-Prado, Gesine. *Sugar Baby: Confections, Candies, Cakes & Other Delicious Recipes for Cooking with Sugar.* Stewart, Tabori & Chang, 2011.

Chattman, Lauren. *Icebox Cakes.* The Harvard Common Press, 2007.

Colwin, Laurie. *Home Cooking: A Writer in the Kitchen.* Vintage, reprint 2010.

Colwin, Laurie. *More Home Cooking: A Writer Returns to the Kitchen*. Harper Perennial, 2000.

Davidson, Alan. *The Oxford Companion to Food, 2nd Ed.* Oxford University Press, 2010.

Grigson, Jane. *Good Things*. Grub Street Cookery, reprint 2008.

Kimball, Christopher. *The Dessert Bible*. Little, Brown and Company, 2000.

Librarie Larousse. *Larousse Gastronomique: The World's Greatest Culinary Encyclopedia, Completely Revised and Updated*. Clarkson Potter, Rev. 2009.

McGee, Harold. *On Food and Cooking: The Science and Lore of the Kitchen*. Scribner, Rev. 2004.

Palm, Michelle. *Jelly Shot Test Kitchen: Jell-ing Classic Cocktails—One Drink at a Time*. Running Press, 2011.

Saulsbury, Camilla V. *No-Bake Cookies: More Than 150 Fun, Easy & Delicious Recipes for Cookies, Bars, and Other Cool Treats Made Without Baking*. Cumberland House Publishing, 2006.

Spencer, Colin. *BRITISH FOOD: An Extraordinary Thousand Years of History*. Grub Street Cookery, reprint 2011.

FRIENDS ONLINE AND BEYOND

Maureen Abood - maureenabood.com

Victoria Belanger - jellomoldmistress.com

Monica Bhide - monicabhide.com

Dorie Greenspan - doriegreenspan.com

David Leite - leitesculinaria.com

Nancie McDermott – nanciemcdermott.com

Domenica Marchetti – domenicacooks.com

Lynne Olver – foodtimeline.org

Anjali Prasertong – eatyrgreens.com

Elizabeth Besa Quirino - asianinamericamag.com

Maria Speck – mariaspeck.com

ACKNOWLEDGMENTS AND THANKS

This book, like all cookbooks, was made with many hands. I owe sweet thanks to an abundance of people. Special gratitude to Jenni Ferrari-Adler, my agent, who said, "Tell me more about pudding . . ." Thank you deeply to my editor, Natalie Kaire, who so enthusiastically and graciously ushered this book into being. I was delighted to have Stacy Newgent's talent in on this project; her dreamy photographs are pure luxury for me. The same goes for Amy Sly's lively, bright design—not to mention the styling expertise of Simon Andrews and Deborah Williams. Thank you for making this book so beautiful.

I remember bouncing around ideas for these recipes years ago with Emma Christensen, recipe writer and editor extraordinaire, and I am grateful to her, Sara Kate Gillingham-Ryan, Maxwell Gillingham-Ryan, Cambria Bold, and the rest of the team at The Kitchn, who were patient with me as I was in the throes of finishing this book, and who have done so much to make me a better cook and writer. Dana Velden, Leela Cyd Ross, Megan Gordon, Anjali Prasertong, Stephanie Barlow, Elizabeth Passarella, Emily Ho, Regina Yunghans, Nora Singley, Nora Maynard, Nealey Dozier, Mary Gorman, and Sarah Rae—you inspire every day. And thank you to the readers of The Kitchn, who showed me just how much love there is out there for icebox cakes. I'm truly indebted to you.

I was privileged to attend The Food Writers' Symposium in the autumn of 2011, and the food professionals I met there have been so generous and warm in their mentorship and advice—I can't thank you enough for the gifts of your wisdom and friendship. Grace Young, Dorie Greenspan, Maureen Abood, Nancie McDermott, Monica Bhide, Francis Lam, Jess Thomson, and many more. Above all, David Leite and Antonia Allegra—thank you.

Other friends and sweet inspirations I must thank include Jeni Britton Bauer, Lynne Olver of the incredible Food Timeline, Victoria Belanger, Domenica Marchetti, Elizabeth Besa Quirino, and Maria Speck. I love and appreciate my hometown friends Rachel Tayse Baillieul, Robin Davis, Shelley Mann, Bethia Woolf, and Kristen Schmidt. Let's have a pudding party soon.

Thank you to my friends at The Thing, who gladly ate pudding, jellies, and icebox cakes week after week, and to my one-of-a-kind family—Mom, Dad, Jed, Susanna, David and Debs, Ann Marie, Daniel and Ruthie, Stephen and Summer, and Paul—thanks for cheering me on.

And, last but not least, wholehearted gratitude to my husband, Mike, who washed many milk-encrusted pots, sweetly and happily.

INDEX

Note: Page numbers in *italics* refer to illustrations.